The Deal 2024

The Plot to Save America

by

B.A. Kindman

DEDICATION

This Book is dedicated to the children of the Next Generation, whatever they may call you. Please remember that you really can change the world if you focus on changing one mind at a time, starting with your own.

TABLE OF CONTENTS

Chapter One
CAMELOT VS. KAMALALOT

"When the government fears the people, there is liberty. When the people fear the government, there is tyranny"

- Thomas Jefferson

What if everything that you have been told during the 2024 Election Season has been a lie? What if the real threat to Democracy comes, as History has taught us, from the Left and not from the Right? See for example, the famous reprint of Friedrich A. Hayek's *The Road to Serfdom* in cartoon format in Appendix I of this Book. The goal of the Left has always been to curb the freedom of the people in order to provide for the people. The goal of the Constitution (as well as the Declaration of Independence) has always been to limit the intrusions of the Government into the "Life, Liberty, and the Pursuit of Happiness" of the People as they strive to form "a more Perfect Union". The conflict between these two ways of thinking has never been more apparent, and once again the Election of 2024 is being called the "Election of Our Lifetime". This Book is being written for the Generation yet unborn so that they might understand how Social Security collapsed in 2034 and the Government collapsed under its out-of-control debt in 2036.

Take for instance the case of Peter Zeihan, the noted Author and Geopolitical Expert. Whenever he walks into a room – no matter where he is – he normally becomes the "Smartest Guy" in that room. Prior to one of his many trips outside of the United States to speak somewhere, Zeihan himself predicted that Joe Biden would win this election. His assessment was very logical as 40% of registered voters are registered as Independents, 32% are registered as Democrats, and 28% are registered as Republicans. Zeihan makes the point that of the 40% of the voters that call themselves "Independent" most still vote for the same party 90% of the time – leaving only 10% of the 40% group as truly "Independent". He states that he is one of those "true" Independents – but that there are very few of them. We believe that this upcoming election of 2024 will come down to less than 100,000 Americans in seven "battleground" states that have determined the Electoral College winner in the last two presidential elections, Hillary's loss in 2016 and Biden's victory in 2020. The same trend will play out in our predicted defeat of the Kamala Harris campaign in 2024.

We were going to start this Book saying we were "life- long" Republicans who supported other Republicans rather than Trump, but when faced with the absolute threat that Kamala represents to the Republic, we believe that "the Devil you know is better than the Devil you don't" … Right?

But actually, the truth is that we are "life-long" Catholics like Joe Biden. No one is truly a "life-long" Republican or Democrat, and now most of us are recent Independents. You are baptized a Catholic before you can speak, and your Godparents must speak for you, whereas you only become a member of a Political Party when you register to vote at age 18.

So what happened to America? Most Americans are searching for Camelot – wise leaders trained at Harvard and baptized by the fire of war who will make the right decisions for the American public without favoring their own family. Now we have someone running for office who was a teacher and literally bragged that none of his students went to Yale, as if going to Yale – like both Hillary and Bill Clinton did – was somehow a bad thing.

This is important because a "bad man" Richard Nixon won an election landslide over a "good man" 52 years ago in 1972. Richard Nixon would resign in 1974 and the word "Watergate" came into the American vocabulary permanently. How could such a "popular" President leave in disgrace in such a short period of time?

Joe Biden was also summarily dismissed by the real powers that control the Democratic Party. Those people rigged the primaries so Biden would win and then rigged the election so Kamala would not lose the millions already donated by loyal Democrats. So in two presidential elections, Trump has had over 140,000,000 Americans vote for him, but Kamala dropped out before the 2020 Primaries and was installed after the 2024 Primaries. Thus, as it stands now, no American actually voted for her to be President.

This actually happened in 2016, where the Democrats rigged

it so Hillary Clinton would win, and she literally became the only Democrat that Trump could beat. So once again, roughly 100,000 voters in six states (seven if you add North Carolina which is close as well) will determine who is the next President. We have never met anyone who is "pro-abortion" or "anti-life", but one would think that was what the entire 2024 Election was solely all about, after the Supreme Court unwisely and needlessly overturned *Roe v. Wade* in the Dobbs Opinion. Social Security and Medicare are facing dramatic cuts and Kamala wants to add 87,000 IRS hires to make the Rich pay their fair share. Trust us, the Rich do not pay any taxes; just ask Peter Thiel and Mitt Romney about their Roth IRAs. But those 87,000 new IRS hires will all need to be paid and they will all be provided with Government Pensions and post-retirement healthcare – both of which are largely unavailable to regular American workers in the private sector. Like most things in Washington, hiring large numbers of new people into the IRS will only add to the record Two-Trillion per Year budget deficit – and the IRS hires will have their pensions paid despite the cuts in Social Security and Medicare coming in 2034.

In 2024, Freedom of Speech is under attack by the Government. One former President has had his home raided in a bogus search for Government documents allegedly in his possession illegally, and with a defective search warrant where the search warrant affidavit was not attached as required by law; while another President had demonstrably greater quantities of these types of documents, stored in the garage of his private residence right out in the open next to one of his cars.

Strange words like "lawfare" have replaced "Watergate" in the public discourse, and one Party is counting on Americans to be stupid while the other Party is hoping most Americans will see through the lies. One Party wants the people to ignore what they see, while the other Party hopes people will wake up in time to perceive the unfolding disaster before it is too late. So, we are writing this Book for the future generations in the hope that it is not too late to save America.

Chapter Two
WHY HILLARY REALLY LOST

"Every country has the government it deserves"

- Joseph de Maistre

We will leave it to the folks at the Democratic National Committee (DNC) to figure out how they lost Wisconsin by a mere 22,748 votes in 2016, when not a single poll predicted a win by President Trump in Wisconsin and the Democrats had won that state in every presidential election since 1984. So, how could they possibly lose to someone that the Wisconsin Republican Party did not even want visiting their state? (Remember, Paul Ryan cancelled Trump's invitation to Wisconsin in October 2016 when the Billy Bush recording went viral). Could it be that Hillary lost Wisconsin because she was the first and only Democratic candidate in 40 years to have not set foot in Wisconsin during the campaign, much less actively campaigned there? While we will leave it to the DNC to figure out what happened in Wisconsin, on the other hand, we will tell you exactly how Hillary lost Michigan by 10,000 votes and Pennsylvania by 45,000 votes. Minority voters stayed home because they remembered that it was Bill Clinton who signed into law the infamous 1994 "Crime Bill" (originally sponsored by Joe Biden), which began the mass incarceration of minorities in America for non-violent drug offenses.

The Crime Bill of 1994, known as the "Violent Crime Control and Law Enforcement Act" of 1994, put more cops on the streets, increased prison budgets, and made "Mandatory Minimums" a part of the new legal lexicon. Many articles have been written by the New York Times and Wall Street Journal and others on how Clinton's Crime Bill began the destruction of minority families and communities across America. By the time the penalties for drug crimes had been reduced by Amendments to the Sentencing Guidelines in 2015, the damage had already been done.

If you don't believe us, please review just two interesting statistics: in certain neighborhoods of Wayne County Michigan (Detroit), there were zero votes – literally NO VOTES – for the President, yet he won Michigan's Electoral College Electors by a mere 10,000 votes. Also, please compare the minority votes in Wayne County for Barack Obama in 2008 (660,000) with the votes for Hillary in 2016 (520,000), and you will see the difference is not just dramatic, it is staggering. Once again, Jill Stein made no difference in Detroit or Philadelphia, where Hillary really lost the election. Second, please recall that Jared Kushner's polling analytics group in Texas (none of whom are from Russia) knew where Hillary was weak and where the President should concentrate his campaigning in the final days, while Hillary had to be told by President Obama's people that she needed to end the campaign in Philadelphia. Obviously, some people in the Obama Camp or the DNC knew that Hillary was losing the minority vote in Philadelphia, which easily could have swept the suburban parts of Pennsylvania that went heavily for the President like, for example, the rural-industrial area around Scranton (Joe Biden's hometown).

So, why would the Clinton Crime Bill of 1994 be so bad for minority communities in America that they would remember it a generation later, and then stay home and risk President Trump winning the election rather than vote for a Party that had long taken their vote for granted? After all, "What have you got to lose?" Think of a two-ounce bag of Cheetos in a vending machine at work; it is a very small bag in a vending machine. But, if that two-ounce bag was filled with "crack" cocaine instead of Cheetos, the person could get 20 years in prison under the Sentencing Guidelines as amended by the Clinton Crime Bill and other "tough on crime" bills passed during the Clinton era that the President's Attorney General Jeff Sessions seemed to favor as well.

Former Attorney General Jeff Sessions refused to de-criminalize marijuana, and actually wanted to revoke the Cole Memorandum drafted by former Acting Attorney General James Cole, who suggested that the federal authorities have more important things to do than waste their time prosecuting and incarcerating drug dealers. Luckily for the President, Attorney General Sessions was replaced by perhaps the best Attorney General of all time, William Barr. In any event, most Americans do not realize that two ounces is more than 50 grams, which can qualify you for 20 years or longer in prison depending on the drug. Even more bizarre, and we know this is hard to believe, but there are people in federal prison for allegedly being in a conspiracy to sell "synthetic marijuana," which only became a Schedule One drug temporarily, and is not as harmful as the notorious K2, which is still being sold in many corner stores and bodegas to this day. The Sentencing Guidelines make "synthetic" marijuana 167 times more criminal by weight than "real" marijuana, which of course is now legal in most states but not by the Federal Government. So, if you are caught with just an ounce of "synthetic" marijuana, your sentence by weight will be 167 times more severe than if you were caught by former Attorney General Jeff Sessions himself in Alabama with "real" marijuana. Can you imagine how people feel about their minority family and friends serving 10-20 years for marijuana (or even worse, "synthetic" marijuana), when in many states real marijuana is legal medically or recreationally, if not completely decriminalized?

Additionally, and perhaps another compelling reason for Hillary's loss, there are a number of recent studies in the ongoing debate over NAFTA that show NAFTA caused the loss of over one million American jobs, most of which were high- paying jobs in Michigan and the surrounding states in the automobile industry. Generally, these were high-paying Union jobs, but specifically, they were high-paying jobs with great benefits provided by the UAW health and welfare benefit plans. Most of these plans were gutted after the bankruptcy of General Motors, and virtually right after the signing of NAFTA in 1994, those jobs left Michigan, Indiana, and Wisconsin. NAFTA also exacerbated the income inequality in America, as the Wealthy could rely on cheap labor in Mexico to make the products they would then sell in America, without worrying about trade tariffs. Just as with the Crime Bill, the President that stabbed organized labor in the back was not a Republican, but rather a Democrat who claimed he could "feel the pain" of the Poor and the people put out of work by the alleged "evil" acts of the previous Republican Presidents in the name of free trade.

Studies have also shown that huge blocks of Democrats in the industrial towns of states affected by NAFTA like Wisconsin, Indiana, Michigan, and Pennsylvania, voted first for Bernie Sanders in the primaries, but then voted for President Trump in the general election, rather than voting for another Clinton that would sell them down the river. It is amazing how many so-called "Free-Trade" Republicans were shocked by what President Trump did, while lifetime solid "Blue-Collar" Democrats support him in tearing up all of the NAFTA-like trade agreements and implementing new and more beneficial trade agreements with our trade partners. One could certainly argue that Indiana would have gone for the President in any event because the Vice President was a former popular governor there. One could also argue that if former Vice President Joe Biden could not save Scranton and the surrounding towns in Pennsylvania for the Democrats, no one could. But NAFTA caused the loss of a number of manufacturing jobs in Wisconsin and absolutely devastated Michigan, and it was a Clinton that signed NAFTA into law.

While our thesis remains that Hillary lost the election because her husband decimated the lives of the minority communities across America, especially in cities like Detroit and Philadelphia with the Crime Bill of 1994, it is also quite possible that hardworking longtime Democratic white males who lost their jobs due to Bill Clinton signing NAFTA into law also said "We won't be fooled again." Certainly that explains the outcome in Wisconsin, where Hillary did not campaign and was the only Democratic presidential candidate to lose Wisconsin since 1984.

The election records show that many White Male Democrats voted for President Trump over Hillary in Indiana, but that did not make the difference in the election outcome and President Trump probably would have won Indiana anyway. That makes the evidence overwhelming that what truly cost Hillary the election was the slight edge of votes that President Trump received in Wisconsin, Pennsylvania, and most of all in Michigan which suffered the most from the two devastating bills signed into law by her husband: NAFTA and the Crime Bill. So, while it is true that Jill Stein received 51,463 votes in Michigan and 31,006 votes in Wisconsin (both tallies were greater than President Trump's margin of victory), there were also more than 87,000 people in Michigan that voted for people lower on the ballot, but not for President Trump or Hillary. And, of course, more than one- third of the registered voters in Michigan stayed home altogether and did not vote. Therefore, one of the reasons for this Book is to get all Americans to leave the "Do-Nothing Party" and get involved in this most important election of our lifetime.

The true danger to the Republic does not come from who occupies the White House, but who occupies the "Deep State" contained in the FBI, the Justice Department, and even the FISA Court. If unlawful and unconstitutional search warrants can be issued by "rubber stamps" of "probable cause" by magistrate judges, in secret, in order to go after the "President's Men" then no one in America is truly safe. Roger Stone's home was invaded by more armed federal agent "commandos" than took out Osama bin Laden in May 2011. His alleged crime was lying to Congress. On the other hand, Representative Adam Schiff has repeatedly lied to Congress and is still lying to the American people in covering up the "Crossfire Hurricane" secret investigation, which violated all concepts of Due Process and was truly designed to interfere with the American election process. Like most criminals, Representative Schiff committed several crimes in a conspiracy with others and then blamed innocent parties in order to coverup his and his co-conspirators' crimes. That is the real danger to the Republic; not President Trump.

Chapter Three
THE RISE OF THE DO-NOTHING PARTY

"We in America do not have government by the majority. We have government by the majority who participate."

- Thomas Jefferson

In the mid-19th Century, particularly from 1850-1860, the American Party – better known to history as the "Know Nothing" Party – flourished in certain parts of the Country. The name "Know Nothing" had nothing to do with the members' intelligence or mental acuity; it was more of a secret society or a fraternity with the same strict rules of nondisclosure as the fictional *"Fight Club"* where if members were asked if they belonged to the American Party, they were to answer "I know nothing." This could be known today as the Sergeant Schultz Party (of *Hogan's Heroes* fame), but the "Know Nothing Party" was extremely nativistic, xenophobic, and their hatred of German and Irish immigrants was only surpassed by their hatred and distrust of all Catholics. The "Know Nothings" were convinced that the Catholics would lead America to be taken over by the Pope in Rome.

The "Know Nothings" seemed to hate many things, but did not make clear exactly what they stood for or what they actually liked or supported. This failure on their part led to their inevitable downfall, as they did not have a candidate for the election of 1860, and their failure to take a stand on Slavery led to many of their members defecting to the Republican Party of Abraham Lincoln and even a few to the Democratic Party of Andrew Jackson. By 1860, the Federalist Party, the Whigs, and the Jeffersonian Republican Party had all disappeared because the issue of Slavery had become so polarizing. But, the xenophobic and anti-immigrant hatred of the nativistic "Know-Nothings" remains with us in different characteristics, and certainly with different names.

It is difficult to imagine that any contemporary political party today called the "American Party" could be against Women's Suffrage or Racial Equality or be rabidly anti-Irish, anti-Italian, or anti-Catholic and still be taken seriously for that matter. While certainly the White Anglo-Saxon Protestant (WASP) movement has certain protected enclaves of privilege throughout America, no one – even secretly – would come out and say they were anti-Irish, anti-Italian, or anti-Catholic and hope to survive in politics in this day and age. There is a greater chance that such a candidate would be "whacked" by the fictional Mafia character Tony Soprano than to make it to the White House on a campaign of hatred against the Catholics, Irish, Italians, and Germans. That said, maybe a campaign of hate could still win as long as it is against immigrants (who will steal our jobs), Muslims (who are "terrorists" that do not share our religion), and the Chinese who are "stealing" from us because they manufacture certain products better and cheaper than we do. The names have changed, but the game is the same: ignite and inflame ethnic hatred for political advantage. The wealthy and well-off tell the Common Man to fear the Mexican immigrant who is willing to face death in trying to come to America to create a better life for his family simply because that immigrant will allegedly "take" jobs that most Americans are not willing to do.

The same ethnic hatred allows our universities to have more Chinese and Indian students than anywhere else in the World, while at the same time we make it more difficult for these well-educated students to get citizenship here. Now that Vietnam has surpassed China as our "favorite" trading partner and handled the Coronavirus Pandemic better than any large country, and President Trump saw fit to meet with North Korea's President in Vietnam, we should all remember that Ho Chi Minh was at one time living and working in America. How many lives could have been saved in the Vietnam War if we did not "fear" all Communists? What if we could learn to embrace all people regardless of race, religion, or nationality?

This leads us to the "Know Nothings" of the present day; the new "Do Nothing" Party. There are more Americans in the "Do Nothing" camp than Democrats and Republicans combined. Too many Americans live paycheck to paycheck, and they only become political if for some reason their government check does not come in the mail or does not clear. Politics to them is not even a game or a pastime. They have more interest in the local sports team than they do in the people running – and ruining – their lives and Country. The purpose of this Book is to wake up the sleeping American masses who are sitting on their collective duffs while certain financially- motivated political forces are stealing their country from under their collective noses. Over 100 million people who were eligible to vote in the 2016 election did not do so.

There are about 130 million people affected by the out-of-control mass incarceration in this country. Too many American families have been hurt by ridiculous laws and excessive and oppressive mandatory minimum sentences that lead to horrifying results. In 1969, there were 25,000 people in federal prisons. Now, 50 years later, there are 180,000 which is down from 225,000 just a few years ago, and yet we still have more prisoners in America than any developed nation in the World. We have only 4% of the World's population, but 25% of the World's prison population. We have ruined our youth with phony foreign wars, mortgaged our grandchildren's future with ballooning debt, bankrupted our children with virtually unpayable student loans, and mortgaged our own financial future with ever-increasing "defense" spending in a military-industrial complex operating with near impunity that President Eisenhower warned us about. This is before the Coronavirus Pandemic of 2020. We also have 25% of the World's deaths from COVID-19.

In the 1960s America fought a war on poverty, but in many

respects, poverty is even worse today than it was then. People should not be without basic healthcare, and children in America should not go to bed hungry or become obese. In the 1970s America fought a war on crime, but that only seemed to take away many of our civil rights, and we certainly are not safer today than we were then. In the 1980s America fought a war on drugs, and not only did the drugs win the war, many Americans lost their freedom or their lives, and all Americans lost even more civil rights and liberties.

In the 1990s America fought yet another war on crime with the Crime Bill of 1994 which we will discuss later in this Book, but this one Act led to the incarceration of millions, and the loss of liberty for everyone else. By the time the 21st Century dawned upon us, we Americans were woken from our peaceful slumber by the Tumbling Towers of 9/11. Suffice it to say that the Patriot Act and the War on Terror stripped away any semblance of liberty or freedom in America and replaced it with equal incarceration of rich and poor alike.

While we deride Russia and North Korea and believe that George Orwell's 1984 is a work of fiction rather than prophecy, the Founding Fathers would shudder at what their beautiful Constitution has turned into in this "Kafkaesque nightmare" that is today's America. Read Thomas Jefferson's words from the Declaration of Independence in the beginning of this Book. Does anyone truly believe that anyone in Washington governing our country believes those words apply today? While *Hamilton* could become the most popular musical of all time, what would the real Alexander Hamilton think about America today?

That is why this Book is a call to action: The time to hesitate, talk, or procrastinate is over. We are no longer talking about Social Security and Medicare being bankrupt in 2030 or 2038, we are saying that Climate Change is certainly not a hoax, but a reality and an emergency that cannot be ignored any longer. There are now only two types of intelligent people writing about Climate Change: those who think it is too late and we are doomed to destruction, and those who believe if we act now we can save the Earth in the next 20-30 years; but only if we act now. Ignore all of the billionaires who want to go to Mars or take trips into space. If you have ever read a science book in your life, please wake up because the truth is out there. If you still don't believe Climate Change is real, ask anyone with a home on the coast in Rhode Island or in a burned-out forest in California.

So, if people want to hold on to their "coal-digging" jobs, why not give each coal family a $100,000 tax-free transfer grant to go to Nevada and mine Lithium instead? Medicare for all will not work, because 135 million people like their current health insurance. The problem with Obamacare is that it did not add a single nurse or doctor to aid the poor; it only made insurance company executives rich. If you don't believe us, Mark Bertolini of Aetna received a $500 million payout on the CVS acquisition of Aetna, and David Wichmann of UnitedHealth received millions in compensation and had a net worth of $340 million.

Once again, Obamacare just required Americans for the first time in history to buy an expensive product that people did not want to buy while eliminating the more beneficial and cost-effective products, doctors, and networks that the people wanted to be in. There were no new doctors or nurses for the poor. People needed access to free healthcare, but instead they got expensive health insurance that they could not afford with high deductibles that could not take care of them and that they could not pay. Ironically, most of today's bankruptcies are caused by exorbitant hospital bills that are not covered by Obamacare. If for no other reason than that, you must declare your "Independence" by leaving the "Do-Nothing" Party and getting active on one of these pressing issues before it is too late.

Chapter Four
A FALSE SENSE OF SOCIAL SECURITY

- James Russell Lowell

Any Government study that you read on the subject will predict that both Social Security and Medicare will run out of money sometime between 2030 and 2040. Certainly, there are a number of solutions to the problem such as increasing contributions to the program Trust Funds by high-income earners (please do not use the term "Lock Box" which sounds more like a device used by a bank in a Debtor's Prison rather than providing security for the Elderly in America), or by cutting the benefits to some of the most vulnerable people in our society. So far, the political "will" has been to cut benefits for the needy at the same time taxes are cut for the wealthiest among us, which explains why in just one generation from 1991 to 2016, the number of bankruptcies for people over the Age of 65 has tripled. How could this happen in the space of 25 years? The answer is easy to discover with very little academic research.

Since the early 1990s, income for most Americans has

remained flat while expenses have gone up and the savings rate has gone down, and the interest rate paid on the little money that is saved is close to zero. While American incomes have remained relatively stagnant over the past 40 years, or gone down considerably in certain industries, most living expenses have gone up steadily over the same time period with Healthcare for the Old and Education for the Young rising dramatically each and every year. The so-called "Baby-Boomers" became a "sandwich generation" that had to figure out how to pay for Long Term Care for Mom and Dad, while putting a son or a daughter through college, and yet, somehow saving for their own retirement.

The truth is that, except for a small lucky few at the top, everyone in America is up to their eyeballs in debt and no one has saved enough money for retirement because Medicare does not pay for Long Term Care in a nursing home and one bad illness can wipe out a family's lifetime savings. Sadly enough, most Americans do not know how Medicare or Social Security works, and they do not research anything until they get a salmon-colored postcard from the Social Security Administration a few months before their 65th birthday. Most Americans do not know that you need to sign up for Medicare before your 65th Birthday or you can pay a penalty each year for the rest of your life. Significantly, most Senior Citizens are unaware that there are Medicare programs that cost them nothing, and yet provide vital dental, vision, and even prescription drug coverage for free.

Imagine how we feel when we see the story of an elderly woman in America that must choose between paying her rent or paying for her medicine? That should not happen in the richest nation on Earth.

As if that was not bad enough, starting in the early 1980s, many large companies abandoned their traditional pension plans in favor of a new type of plan called a Cash-or-Deferred Savings Plan – now known everywhere by its Internal Revenue Code Section name of 401(k). The companies that did not abandon their pension plans eventually ended up in bankruptcy like the airlines PanAm and Eastern, and of course General Motors, which thanks to its major union the UAW had the best and most expensive post-retirement package ever introduced to the American Worker. Now, however, post-retirement health plans are a rarity and the surviving plans are always running short of funds if they do not end up being terminated in Bankruptcy Court as part of some leveraged buyout that went bad.

So now, within the space of 25-30 years, the retiring American worker has no employer-paid comprehensive post-retirement healthcare coverage and no pension plan, so the typical worker has no post-retirement security and cannot make ends meet on a meager Social Security check. At least once each week, the nightly news features a story about some poor homeless veteran that cannot afford to pay for his prescription drug medicines because Medicare Part D prohibits the United States government from negotiating lower prescription drug costs for Americans even if they happen to be homeless veterans.

Millions of American families are living in fear that they are one car repair or broken refrigerator away from being unable to pay their bills or being homeless and living in poverty. But the Veterans Administration has 400,000 people working on the government payroll who get pensions and healthcare benefits paid for by the American people.

It is bad enough that America won World War II with only 200,000 employees in all branches of government, but now the Veterans Administration has grown so large that even an Admiral in the Navy who was the doctor for the President was not qualified to run the Veterans Administration because it is so large. How quickly America forgets that a mere "community organizer" ran the Country for eight years and increased the government payroll from 2,000,000 employees working for the government to nearly 5,000,000 employees. Once again, most of those extra employees working for the government will receive generous pension and medical benefits that the actual Veterans and the Elderly do not receive. Yet, when the President announced that there would be a hiring freeze and no automatic pay increase for federal workers, the Democrats and the federal workers – "servants" of the People – erupted in anger. But wait, it gets worse.

Remember that the Government's own actuaries report every year that the Social Security Trust Fund and Medicare are running out of money, and long before the Coronavirus, the Congressional Budget Office said in 2017 that, while our National Debt was already at $22 trillion, we were doomed to live with annual trillion- Dollar deficits for years to come and soon the interest on the National Debt will take more money than things like the Defense or Medicare budgets. Prior to the Coronavirus Pandemic of 2020, spending by Congress was already out of control, and no one in Washington seems to care. In fact, the actual indebtedness for the Government is over $70 trillion because there are a lot of items that are carried "Off Balance Sheet," like the future pension and other post-retirement benefit expenses for all of those people that work for the Government that have both health insurance and pension plans, while many ordinary American workers in the Private Sector have neither.

The pension and health insurance benefits for the ever-increasing number of government employees is paid for by the American taxpayers, and while taxes for the Wealthy are reduced, the average government worker and elected politicians have better and better benefits while the "Safety Net" for the Poor and Elderly becomes more and more frayed each year. It should not be a surprise to anyone that the Maryland and Virginia suburbs surrounding the Capital have become among the wealthiest enclaves in America, while both rural Americans and inner-city Americans get progressively and relatively poorer each year.

Recently, a distinguished economics professor from Boston

was quoted on Russian Television (of all places) saying that America's "off-balance sheet" debt was actually in the range of $225 trillion, not the mere $35 trillion that most politicians rant and rave about, yet do nothing to change or reduce. The International Institute of Finance located in Washington, D.C. has estimated that the entire world debt has gone up to $250 trillion from $233 trillion last year, and $217 trillion the year before that. So, probably, America's "off-balance sheet" debt is only about $150 trillion rather than the $225 trillion the distinguished Boston professor told the Russians. Either that, or American families owe about 90% of the entire World Debt. But every American should look at the lower right-hand corner of the famous Debt Clock for America's "Unfunded Liabilities." See Debt Clock at https://www.usdebtclock.org/.

But, whatever the number, each and every young American is literally "drowning" in debt. Congress figured out a long time ago that the best way to secure the votes of today is to saddle future generations with an unpayable debt. After all, unborn children cannot vote, nor do they attend protest rallies. Worst of all, the feckless politicians running the biggest Ponzi-scheme in history will all be dead when the children of the next generation come of age and realize what was done to them by their parents and grandparents (Perhaps you?).

Not only is this kind of debt unsustainable, the type of income inequality that exists in America today is also unsustainable. During the past 40 years from 1977 to 2019, arguably the greatest years in American financial history, over 60% of the increased wealth went to less than 1% of the American population while at the same time real wages for everyone else has remained stagnant or decreased based on inflation. Also, costs for everyone have gone up, but the taxes paid by the wealthiest individuals and corporations have consistently gone down starting with the Tax Reform Act of 1976 and the new Internal Revenue Code of 1986. The concentration of wealth and power in the hands of a few American families has never been greater, and has worsened during the Coronavirus Pandemic of 2020.

Therefore, one of the purposes of this Book is to educate you on this disparity. The Wealthy do not pay their "fair share" of taxes and neither should you. The Wealthy do everything they possibly can to provide for a secure retirement for their families, and so should you. Hopefully, this Book will help you and your family do just that. In the meantime, get active, get registered, and drive a friend or two to the local polling booth this November. For once, please vote like your entire future depends on it.

Chapter Five
THE AMERICAN OLIGARCHS

"We must make our choice. We may have democracy, or we may have wealth concentrated in the hands of a few, but we can't have both."

- Justice Louis Brandeis

Please read the statement below, and try to guess what year it was written in describing the American economy, and the problem with the unequal distribution of wealth in the hands of a few families:

"One percent of American families control more of the general wealth than the remaining ninety-nine percent. There are 6,700 companies with a capitalization of thirty-six billions of dollars and an actual property estimated to be worth twenty-seven billions, or sixty percent of all the wealth of the United States outside of farm value and city values in residences and in private businesses. The statement that the business of the country is controlled by less than 100 men - aye by a mere handful of men - requires the citation of no authority further than the list of transportation, industrial, and financial trusts, combinations and corporations of the country. The official records of those institutions are in themselves the proof. Six men in America today could stop the wheels of all the most important industries. Fifteen million American wage earners receive less than [] dollars a year." *

Similarly, Citigroup published a famous whitepaper describing how America had become a Plutocracy (control by the wealthiest), not an Aristocracy (control by the "best"). In October of 2005, Citigroup Research Analyst Ajay Kapur wrote a fascinating and informative report of the growing disparity of wealthy and income in the United States, entitled *Plutonomy: Buying Luxury, Explaining Global Imbalances*. The gist of Kapur's analysis is that the United States (and a few other wealthy nations) had become a Plutocracy with the concentration of wealth and power in a few hands; so much so that Citigroup's investment clients would be wise to focus only on those companies that cater to the rich. (See *Plutonomy*, Citigroup, Ajay Kapur, CFA, October 16, 2005).

Mexico or China were misplaced, and in fact the entire world economy was "being held up by the muscular arms of its entrepreneur-plutocrats, like it or not." More than a decade later, Plutonomy is still a good read and is spot-on with its predictions that there will be a continuing struggle between free-trade economists and those who seek to limit immigration and impose tariffs. Kapur also cites to the arguments that Kevin Phillips made in his book Wealth and Democracy, where he points to the demise of the Netherlands as a world power in the late 1700's due to the increasing obsession with financial speculation, which caused "non-financial skilled labor that had built the country's wealth to seek their success in other countries." That same affliction caused Britain to lose its educational dominance after World War I.

---

* See *Concentrated Wealth*, Richard Henry Edwards, 1910, pp. 8-9.

For the purposes of this Book, *Plutonomy* predicts several threats to the Great American Plutocracy by using the analysis of the famous Harvard political and ethical philosopher, John Rawls (see, e.g., *A Theory of Justice*, 1971) who literally created the term "Safety Net" as a moral imperative for a modern society to be dedicated to taking care of its least fortunate. Rawls points out why that is good for Society as a whole, not just the Poor, the Children, and the Elderly. But it is not Rawls' Safety Net that Kapur points to, but rather that the American Plutocracy can be brought down by its own success, or the potential social backlash of the have-nots. Kapur cites Rawlsian analysis to suggest that the "invisible hand" of Adam Smith stops working at some point and no longer functions.

In America, the "Plutocracy" has been allowed to flourish because a number of people in the electorate feel that one day they can become part of the Great American Plutocracy. So, why kill it off when you can join it, which is the embodiment of the "American Dream"… Right? But if enough voters feel they cannot participate in the "Plutocracy" - or get their share of the "wealth pie" - they will vote to divide up the pie instead. In concluding how the Great American Plutocracy might come to an end, Kapur concludes his brilliant whitepaper with the following observations that are critical to some of the themes in this Book:

Our overall conclusion is that a backlash against plutonomy is probable at some point. However, that point is not now. So long as economies continue to grow, and enough of the electorates feel that they are benefiting and getting rich in absolute terms, even if they are less well off in relative terms, there is little threat to plutonomy in the [United States]. Unfortunately for the American Oligarchs, the time of the Great America Plutocracy might be running out, as it is hard to find anyone that still believes in the American Dream. Most people that you speak to feel the "game" is rigged.

Perhaps most disturbing is that this generation will be the first in American history since the signing of the Declaration of Independence where parents will worry that their children may not have a better standard of living than the one they enjoyed. Lifespans in America are getting shorter, not longer; Liberty and personal freedoms are being curtailed, and the "Pursuit of Happiness" is some arcane notion that will someday merely be the name of a video game. While almost everyone in America knows someone who has been hurt (or killed) by COVID-19, American Media has been transfixed on the rapidly increasing wealth (and antics) of Tesla's Elon Musk and Amazon's Jeff Bezos. As Apple stock crosses the $3 trillion mark for the first time, the Biblical adage from Matthew that "the Rich get richer and the Poor get poorer" seems to be truer than ever before.

Chapter Six
THE VELOCITY OF MONEY

"I believe that banking institutions are more dangerous to our liberties than standing armies."

- Thomas Jefferson

Virtually no one in Congress understands the importance of the Velocity of Money to the health of the American economy, or the future of its citizens. If you do not believe that, just search for any speech made by any Senator or Congressman (forget the President) discussing the Velocity of Money during the Coronavirus Pandemic. Why should you be concerned? Because the Velocity of Money as measured by the Federal Reserve is the lowest that it has been since the Great Depression. A chart showing the Velocity of Money in 2018 is virtually identical to the Velocity of Money chart leading up to the depths of the Great Depression in 1932. The current chart for 2020 is even worse, and the Velocity of Money is at the lowest rate in 60 years.

When an economy gets into trouble, the government can either increase debt to buy goods and services to stimulate the economy, or it can do things to stimulate the Velocity of Money in order to revive the economy. In the Great Recession of 2008, the government believed that it had to bail out big corporations and big banks that caused the problem, and the Economy took on great amounts of debt, which created a "Moral Hazard" on Wall Street, so that investment bankers could keep the profits from their good bets private, but share their bad bets and debts with the public. We as a nation are still suffering the effects of Wall Street keeping their profits private and making their debts our children's and their children's responsibility, and it is happening again with the Coronavirus Pandemic.

Despite the complexity of most Federal Reserve formulas, the Velocity of Money is relatively simple. A low rate of the Velocity of Money leads to a "liquidity trap" - where the blood in the system freezes, or the oil that lubricates the engine disappears, because people hoard money rather than spend it. Whichever metaphor you prefer, the result is the same: the economy stalls and a recession or depression ensues. That is why you should be very concerned that the Federal Reserve's Velocity of Money Chart for 2018 looks a lot like the chart leading up to the Great Depression. In fact, the rate for the Velocity of Money for 2017 and 2018 is the lowest it has been since the Great Depression and the Velocity of Money Chart for 2020 is even lower. It is at the lowest level in 60 years. So, what causes a "low" Velocity of Money and what can be done to cure it?

When the people with all the money – the veritable lifeblood of the economy – hoard that money, everyone suffers. Therefore, we need to encourage the wealthy people and corporations to spend their money over and over again as rapidly as possible rather than hoard it or save it as they are currently. If the Wealthy keep all of their money in the stock market, say in Apple stock (see recent chart for AAPL), their wealth increases as Apple's stock increases. And, if Apple as a company keeps all of its money offshore and untaxed (see recent Apple $14 billion victory over the European Union), and borrows money only to buy back its stock, then the only people that benefit are big stockholders like Berkshire Hathaway and the individual shareholders of Berkshire like Warren Buffett. So, while the stock market has hit all-time highs and Apple has become America's first trillion-dollar company (and now two-trillion), and Berkshire has done very well with its large position in Apple, money is not circulating through the economy, and no one is benefiting from this situation other than the shareholders of Apple and Berkshire Hathaway.

Someday everyone will have a cheap smartphone, but we will still have over 50 million people living in poverty, relying on food stamps (SNAP Program), and without health insurance despite the adoption of Obamacare in 2010. Medicare and Social Security are both running out of money, our college students have a trillion-dollar student loan debt, and we have over three million relatively able bodies incarcerated with the taxpayers paying for their expenses while they produce nothing for the economy. The same thing can be said of government employees and their pensions and health insurance paid for by the American Taxpayer.

If Warren Buffett, Berkshire Hathaway, and Apple hoard their money, that is bad for the economy. Sure, you hear people talking about the Fed "lowering the interest rates" so banks will lend more, but we were at zero, and higher interest rates cause people to borrow less resulting in a negative instead of a positive impact on the economy. Tax cuts happen to be the current Administration's favorite option, but that merely increases the Nation's debt and shifts the burden for paying the debt to the next generation. Currently, we have a national debt of over $36 trillion and other "unfunded liabilities" of over $150 trillion, which does not include the unfunded liabilities of all the states or the debts of every household. Just the "unfunded liabilities" amount is more than five times the size of our GDP (Gross Domestic Product), or what we may refer to as our total "sales" or national revenue.

Even assuming that tax cuts provide a stimulus to the economy, which is not always true, America experienced its healthiest economy and lowest debt and balanced budget during the late 1990's because of the "infamous" Bush-Dole tax increase of 1991 that cost Bush 41 the election of 1992. The courage that President Bush and Senator Dole showed in raising taxes while cutting government waste will be shown to be the secret of success for America from 1993-2000, when we last had a balanced budget and no national debt.

Now though, cutting taxes on the wealthiest among us is a fool's errand, because neither the Wealthy nor America's biggest corporations pay their fair share of taxes anyway. When corporate taxes are cut as they have been by the President, it does not stimulate the economy. Instead, it simply allows companies to buy back their stock, making management richer and the shareholders richer. When the stock price of Apple increases due to the tax cut, neither Apple nor its shareholders (like Berkshire Hathaway) pay any taxes on the increase in their wealth. And, the generous companies like AT&T that gave their employees a one-time $1,000 bonus do nothing for the economy other than allowing the employees to buy some new Apple product on Amazon.

So, if lowering or raising interest rates is not the answer, and increasing government debt or lowering taxes could be fatal to America's future, what should the government do to increase the Velocity of Money? There are several articles by well-respected economists on the Internet that suggest a flat tax of 10-20% with no deductions will solve the problem. While a Flat Tax would provide simplicity in its administration, it would not provide the desired effect of having companies buy more things as capital expenditures or hire more people.

More people having good paying jobs would have more money to buy more goods. The more people spend, the more the Velocity of Money increases and the better the economy becomes. The more money that flows, the easier it is to tax someone. If one has an Amazon gift card of $500, and Amazon offers you a book that normally costs $15-$20 at a local bookstore for only $1.99 on Kindle, you will buy the book from Amazon whether you pay 2, 12, or even 18 cents in a National Sales Tax.

The well-educated people that talk about the Value Added Tax utilized so well in Europe forget that most Americans have never heard of or lived under a Value Added Tax system. Yet, if you mention a tax on gasoline, cigarettes, or their phone bill, everyone will understand. If you are a cigarette smoker, you can remember buying a carton of cigarettes for under $10, but now a single pack will cost $10-$12 with most of that increase being tax revenue to the state and local governments and not the increase in the cost of tobacco. Similarly, no local politician has seriously advocated getting rid of the property tax to fund the local schools, even though many people have run a campaign based on that idea. Still, no one has followed through.

Many towns calculate what they need, have the Board of Tax Assessors figure out the value of the property owned in town, and then they set the "Mill Rate" or percentage of tax accordingly based on what the Town needs to pay its bills. No one seems to care that the property tax on their home goes up to $12,000 a year from $6,000 over a ten-year period, as long as the schools are well-run, the streets are safe, and the parks are well-groomed. Only wealthy people have expensive homes, and they have no problem paying property taxes on their various homes to pay the Town's bills.

To the contrary, the states relying heavily on income taxes as well as sales taxes end up losing businesses and their employees to states that are more "business-friendly" (meaning they have lower tax environments). When those income taxes are used to pay pensions for the $100,000 a year lifeguard in California (Google it), the police pensions in Illinois, or the pensions for government employees in Connecticut, most people and businesses find it easy to vote with their feet and move to a lower-tax state. This explains why a governor from Florida will visit Connecticut to recruit businesses for his state, or why Boeing might build a new plant in South Carolina as opposed to Washington.

The best type of tax is one that is relatively painless and completely hidden. Poor people do not buy million dollar homes, so if someone wants to buy a movie star's home in Beverly Hills for $10 million, then they will not hesitate to pay $10.6 million with the 6% tax going to the Federal government. Remember, the California town will collect property taxes each and every year while the Federal government receives money only once on the sale; the same can be said on the sale of an expensive penthouse in New York City to a Russian Oligarch. Currently, when a Russian Oligarch uses an LLC to buy an apartment in one of President Trump's buildings in New York, no money whatsoever goes to the Federal government. Similarly, Apple, Amazon, Tesla, Berkshire Hathaway, Microsoft, Cisco, and Oracle could buy up every company in America by using their stock, and the Federal government would not get a dime in taxes.

The reason for this is IRC §368, which allows a large company to buy a smaller company using its stock through a tax-free merger. Just as real estate tycoons can buy and sell properties tax-free for their entire career by utilizing IRC §1031, so, too, can a company grow even larger by using its stock rather than cash to buy a company, and there is no tax to be paid on either of those two types of transactions. Instead of fighting the merger of AT&T and Time Warner, the Federal government should have taxed it, because even at a tax of 1%, that would be $1 billion to the Federal coffers. Similarly, if Berkshire Hathaway wants to buy Heinz for $20 billion, then it can pay a 1% tax or $200 million for the benefit of buying the company they desire.

Notice that the contest between Disney and Comcast over the assets of Fox provided Rupert Murdoch and his family a tax-free exit from Fox. While Comcast was willing to pay substantially more in cash, neither they nor Disney would blink if it were necessary to pay an additional 1% to the Federal government.

Since most corporate mergers are at a premium, the lucky sellers would probably not protest paying 1% on their good fortune as a "transaction" tax. Once again, anyone fortunate or smart enough to have a large holding in a publicly-traded stock would know how to avoid paying income taxes on the sale of that stock. Just as Vanguard, Fidelity, and Schwab know who to pay the cash to on the sale of the stock, so, too, would they easily know how to collect the 1% security tax from the Sellers. If you doubt this, carefully check your brokerage statements for a security tax that you pay on each trade, almost like a secret commission and also fees collected on dividend payments. This type of tax makes even more sense in the new era of zero-commission trading. Many people were comfortable paying $4.95 per trade. Now that trades are free, though, why not impose a $1.00 per transaction tax to save the World?

Additionally distressing is the fact that if you collect dividends from an old American company that is now operating out of Ireland because of its Inversion, you have to pay a foreign withholding tax as well as an ADR fee, both of which no one told you about and are nonrefundable. It is hard to imagine a company more American than Budweiser or Anheuser Busch (BUD), but now that it is owned by Belgium's InBev, you will pay these tax withholding and ADR fees on that famous "American" stock.

If you purchase 1,000 shares of BUD at $100 per share thinking you will receive $1,000 every quarter based on a 4% dividend, you will be surprised to see the ADR fees and foreign income tax withholding fees will be automatically withdrawn from your account with no hope of recovering these fees that no one ever explained to you. Thus, if our federal government added a modest cost on each dividend distribution, stock trade, or mansion sale, we could painlessly raise billions of dollars from the wealthy to repair the damaged Safety Net in America. That is the proper way to "tax the Rich" while safely increasing the Velocity of Money.

Chapter Seven
TEMPT THE RICH, FEED THE POOR

"The art of government consists in taking as much money as possible from one party of citizens to give to the other."

- Voltaire

Now that you understand the importance of the Velocity of Money, and that the Wealthy do not pay their fair share of taxes while saving their money (read: "hoarding") as evidenced by the dramatic decline in the purchase and prices of expensive homes across the country. Many "millionaire mansions" are 30-40% off their original asking price, which means two terrible things: the Wealthy are selling their expensive homes and are not buying new ones, while hoarding their cash and getting ready for the coming storm (if it is not here already). Whether it is next year or 2026, the "crash" is coming and many say it will be worse than 2008, and possibly rivaling the depths of the Great Depression of 1932.

That said, how can we increase the Velocity of Money without increasing the already dangerous national debt? Everyone knows we need to provide funds for Infrastructure and Healthcare. Increased taxation is not the answer because the Wealthy have shown that they are very resourceful and can legally avoid any taxation year after year. They have the knowledge and the political clout to draft legislation that favors the Wealthy and

America's largest corporations, while not providing necessary funds for infrastructure, health and welfare benefits for the working poor, and food and shelter for the Homeless. Therefore, since the Wealthy control the government, it is up to us to figure out how to provide enough funds to take care of everyone else while providing benefits to the Wealthy that make it worth their while to participate. How can this be done?

First, Congress must repeal IRC Code Sections 141-150, which were added by the new Tax Code of 1986. These Code Sections limit the tax-exempt status of certain types of state and city municipal bonds that were used by private contractors to build things like low-income housing. Believe it or not, some wealthy bankers have gone to prison for being involved with certain types of municipal bonds referred to as "Arbitrage Bonds" despite the fact that these bonds could be the very solution we are looking for to solve the state and municipal debt and Velocity of Money crises in America.

The second deleterious provision in the Tax Code that hurt the economy was to limit each state's issuance of tax-free Private Activity Bonds was raised from $150 million to $311 million (or $105 per capita) for each state. Forget the State's Rights constitutional issue that an agency of the federal government could limit the economy or the borrowing of a state, the IRS and Treasury Regulations on this subject are over 300 pages long just for this part of the Tax Code alone. Not only has this killed the use of municipal bonds by the States to fund their underfunded pension plans with Pension Obligation Bonds, here is a direct quotation from the State of California's own manual from the California Debt and Investment Advisory Commission on the application, sponsorship, and issuance of municipal bonds:

> *"At some point in a bond transaction, take a look at each participant in the deal and decide if you are willing to be a co-defendant with them. If the answer is no, don't do the deal."*

Why would any municipality or state official risk prison time by suggesting a municipal bond deal that might turn sour for some unknown reason in the future? In fact, the "arbitrage" potential of municipal bonds is so powerful and obvious, that the IRS created a tax form to outlaw it and require any arbitrage profits to be sent to the IRS. See Form 8038-T and Code Section 148. The third fatal flaw to tax reform was the addition of Section 265, which prohibited the Banks from getting a tax deduction if they invested in municipal bonds. That meant there would be no good reason for a bank to buy the issuance of a municipality's bond for the Bank's own account when the Federal Reserve wants to create new cash in the system and does Quantitative Easing by buying bonds. It would be great if the Fed could buy city and state municipal bonds, which could then be used to provide for the Poor in the building of free apartments, new schools, and new free health clinics. The "free" apartments must be built by construction companies and managed by people who get paid decent salaries.

A "free" health clinic could be staffed by highly- paid physician assistants and registered nurses who can write prescriptions for CVS or Walmart, and refer serious cases to a local in-network hospital. If that same sick person went to the Emergency Room, they would also be treated for "free", but we would all bear the very expensive cost of treating them in the Emergency Room of a hospital rather than the "free" clinic provided by the funding of municipal bonds by the Federal Reserve. A trip to the Emergency Room could cost as much as $10,000 for a simple procedure that might only cost $100 at the local "free" clinic. Either way, the American Taxpayer will pay for that "free" visit. When the next financial crisis comes, the Central Banks will emulate Japan's Central Bank and buy equities of their biggest companies in order to prop up their individual stock markets.

Hopefully we will be smart enough to invest in small companies and small businesses to make sure the circulation of money is increased and spread out through the economy. To facilitate the repair of the damage done to the American economy by the IRS's misguided attempt to outlaw the use of arbitrage bonds by the municipalities of the various states without any limit, there must be an end to all of these baseless and irrational restrictions in the Tax Code and Regulations, and replace the current system with a new Infrastructure Bank that issues tax-exempt I-Bonds. The new I-Bonds would pay 4% and be exempt from all taxes, including income and estate taxes just like "Flower Bonds" in the post-WWII era. In the post-War period, America benefited from the building of the National Highway System and the benefits of people going to college on the G.I. Bill.

While we all know that it is "very expensive to be poor" in America, with Pay-Day Loans at 400%, credit cards at 20%, car loans at 18%, home loans at 15%, and bank fees and/or bad check fees more than the check itself was written for; it is estimated that there are several hundred thousand people in jail across the Country due to their inability to pay a small amount of bail ($500-$5,000), while on the other hand, wealthy Silicon Valley executives get multi-million-dollar signature loans or home loans at 1.6% to buy their properties. The inequities between the America of the Wealthy and the America of the Poor are readily apparent, but few people in Congress seem to have any inclination to solve these problems and disparities.

A new Infrastructure Bank could be funded solely with 30-year 4% tax-exempt bonds without any government guarantee. Just as with the Federal Reserve, the President could appoint a dozen "governors" or "directors" from across the Country to run the I-Bank. The I-Bank would lend money to city and state agencies for the repair of bridges and roads, and the modernization of airports. Or, it would lend money to private contractors at a cost of 8%, which is relatively low for construction financing, yet would ensure that the private contractor got the project done on time and under budget.

The tax-exempt status of these I-Bonds would encourage well-to-do people from all over the world to invest in a tax-exempt America. Some people actually pay large fees to keep their money in zero interest Swiss Bank accounts. More importantly, civil engineers rate our infrastructure at a D-, and everyone comments that our airports look like they are from a Third-World nation. Thus, the new I-Bank with its newly created tax-exempt I-Bonds would stimulate the economy, increase the Velocity of Money, provide much needed funds to repair our infrastructure at no cost to the American Taxpayer, and give the Wealthy a reason not to hoard their money in the stock market where it is never taxed.

Chapter Eight
THE BEST GOVERNMENT MONEY CAN BUY

"We have the best government that money can buy."

- Mark Twain

Mark Twain's prophetic words describe the terrible situation that we find the Country in right now, because the government is for sale and the buyers willing to pay the highest price are America's largest corporations. Certainly, small businesses and the Poor petition their government for help and services, but their pleas are drowned out by the loud din of America's Lobbyists who have made "wining and dining" into a national pastime, if not a full-fledged industry of its own. The scandals that have erupted in just the past few years have shown that corruption is rampant in Washington, and major companies of major industries are drafting their own legislation for Congress to pass in order to line the pockets of their wealthy shareholders.

In 1976, only 175 corporations had lobbyists and there were only about 300 small Political Action Committees. Of course, there were already associations like the Chamber of Commerce and the National Federation of Independent Businesses, but after Ronald Reagan's election, the number of companies with lobbyists grew to 2,500, and Political Action Committees increased to over 12,000 by 1985. Unsurprisingly, the early

1980s saw the rise of a new type of political consultant/lobbyist in firms like Black, Manafort & Stone, which included the now famous personalities Paul Manafort and Roger Stone.

By 2010, there were over 13,000 registered lobbyists delivering some $4 billion per year to Congress. Providing necessary campaign funds to incumbents in order to assure their re-election was the goal, after all, and those incumbents in turn would favor their generous corporate benefactors. With the Supreme Court's decision in *Citizens United* v. FEC, 558 U.S. 310 (2010), everything changed and the amount of funds that could be secretly funneled to PACs and private interest groups, or even non-profits with patriotic-sounding names, increases each and every year. These organizations can then funnel billions in unregistered money to candidates. According to Forbes, the government's own reports showed the top 200 lobbying organizations from 2007-2012 spent a combined $5.8 billion on federal lobbying and campaign contributions, and that does not include the 13,000 other lobbyists. Forbes calculated that this $5.8 billion resulted in $1.3 trillion in federal business and $3.2 trillion in federal support. This does not include all of the bailouts of the big banks, AIG, or even FNMA. Significantly, according to Forbes, between 2008 and 2010, 29 of America's largest corporations paid no federal taxes on their combined profits of $164 billion. Forbes reported that during this three-year period, these companies spent $476 million on lobbying that created over $11 billion in total tax rebates for only those 29 companies. The financial sector did even better than that.

The largest 49 financial corporations out of the list of 200 invested about $1 billion in campaign contributions and lobbying expenses, and received over $157 billion in federal business and $2.5 trillion in federal support in return. We all know what happened in 2008, which led to the passage of Dodd-Frank and the increased regulation of the Banks. This, of course, led to a dramatic increase in lobbying expenses and campaign contributions. There are numerous articles, book, and even movies decrying the decline of our democracy based on the billions of dollars America's largest corporations contribute to the Clinton Foundation, which raised $500 million while Hillary was Secretary of State; not to mention her famous $250,000 speaking engagements.

The Citizens United decision involved an unflattering movie about Hillary, so it is more than fair that Hillary and the Clinton campaign machine fought fire with fire. The voices seeking campaign reform in Congress were lost in the cacophony of the money-changers in the halls of Congress. There can be no doubt that lobbying dollars infect every aspect of American life, from which drugs Big Pharma pushes the FDA to approve or ban, to the "revolving door" from Congress to the Military Industrial Complex that we were warned about and is still in operation to this day.

The big health insurance carriers helped to draft the

Obamacare legislation, and Big Pharma came up with Medicare Part D program which literally prohibits the government from using its buying power to negotiate the price it pays for drugs. According to the FDA, chemotherapy is "good" for you, yet Vitamin B-17, which is found in the seeds of apples and other fruits like apricots is a better and cheaper "cure" for cancer. Even so, B-17 is not approved for the treatment of cancer by the FDA, and is actually illegal in the form of the drug Laetrile. Why the FDA still bans Laetrile is a mystery, because it is used to treat cancer around the world, including clinics in Mexico and Canada. On the other hand, the FDA has done nothing to ban the manufacture of Fentanyl and other opioids that have caused the death of over 70,000 people in just the last few years.

In all of the clinics worldwide that use B-17 Laetrile to treat cancer, there have been no reported deaths from an "overdose" of B-17, and many oncologists are even using high doses of Vitamin C intravenously to cure cancer. Yet the only approved treatment for cancer by the FDA is the very expensive and unpleasant chemotherapy. So, how much would it cost you to "buy" Congress and change all of that? Obviously, people like the Koch Brothers funding grassroots movements all across America could answer that question.

They became politically active when overzealous government agents and various agencies accused Koch Industries of all sorts of crimes, none of which turned out to be true. But, let's assume that you want to set up a hedge fund to utilize all of your inside business connections on Wall Street, and it is very important that you are never accused of a crime. How much would it cost you to "own" Congress and the legislative machinery and government agencies that Congress controls? For the sake of discussion, let's assume that you call yourself Securities and Commodities Capital, or SAC Capital for short; you have friends in high places and even some relatives that are CEOs of those 29 corporations that make billions yet pay nothing in taxes.

Because you trade on tips from friends at SAC, you want to be very careful that you do not "break" the law, so the prudent thing to do is to "make" the law by paying the right lobbyists and PACs to fund the re-election campaigns of the right Senators and Congressmen. Since a number of Congressmen have been indicted and gone to jail for amounts under $100,000 that were improperly donated or improperly spent, let us assume that $100,000 is all you would need to secure the friendship of a congressman to help you achieve your legislative goals. You only need 218 of the 435 votes in Congress, but shrewd businessman that you are, you make sure to give to seasoned veterans on both sides of the aisle: 120 Democrats and 120 Republicans, all experienced with 3-6 terms or more, and key votes on key committees. At $100,000 per vote, that would cost you $240 million.

Similarly, you only need 60 Senators, and 30 experienced Senators from each party costs about $1 million per Senator. So, now for a mere $300 million you have an effective lock on

Congress and can have your lobbyists whisper in the ears of your friends in Congress how new legislation should be drafted and passed, and how old laws, like those regulating investment banks and keeping them separate from commercial banks, which have worked since the Great Depression, should be amended or done away with altogether.

If you doubt that this $300 million tax-deductible expense is a prudent and inexpensive way for SAC Capital to do business, look at the billion-dollar fines paid by most of the banks in the LIBOR scandal, JPMorgan Chase on the London Whale, and even the $1.8 billion fine paid by the real SAC Capital for failure to monitor its traders. Whether you are a Silicon Valley titan, a Big Pharma CEO, or a Greenwich Hedge Fund manager, it could be well worth your while to employ one of Washington's 13,000 lobbyists or to start your own non- profit PAC.

Lobbying the various agencies of the federal government is a full-time job, involving golf courses, nightclubs, and exotic trips, and is dominated by the largest corporations. Small businesses and average citizens know very little about this high stakes game that affects every aspect of their lives. As stated earlier, less than 1,000 families in America control the purse strings to the lobbyists, and those lobbyists are the ones that hold the keys to Congress. They are the heart and soul of the "Kakistocracy" that James Russell Lowell feared America was turning into, and was desperate to prevent. How about you?

Chapter Nine
WHO KILLED THE FOURTH AMENDMENT?

"The greatest dangers to liberty lurk in insidious encroachment by men of zeal, well-meaning, but without understanding."

- Justice Louis Brandeis

WAKE UP…WAKE UP…WAKE UP! The feds are outside and it is 6:00 A.M. The IRS-CID is outside your door. You are away on business. Your wife, who is also a mother of six, is home alone with your youngest daughter, getting her ready for school. Without warning, two dozen of Obama's "Special Agents" of the IRS-CID (Criminal Investigation Division) break into your house surprising your wife and daughter. Almost all of the IRS Special Agents are large men, heavily armed, with bulletproof vests on. There has been no warning. There has been no Notice of Deficiency, Information Document Request, notice of any audit, audit summons, or any letters from the IRS questioning any tax return that you or your family has ever filed. This true story was covered by most newspapers around the Country between April 13 and 16, 2010 (for example, see Boston.com for just one of the many stories; search for Fort Wayne, IN IRS raid).

This is no mere violation of the Fourth Amendment of the Constitution of the United States, this is an armed commando raid on ordinary Americans; United States citizens. Remember when President Obama was upset that a Boston police officer wrongfully arrested an African- American Harvard professor, and that "misunderstanding" led to beers in the Rose Garden of the White House? How can you feel safe if the homes of the former President Trump and his advisors: Paul Manafort, Michael Cohen, and Roger Stone, were raided with sealed search warrants that were obviously constitutionally and facially defective? How can you feel safe if a young Kentucky woman, Breonna Taylor, was killed in her bed by police invading her home? This Book is written for you in the hope that it is not too late to save the Country from the road that it is currently on.

You must vote Republican in these upcoming Congressional and Senate elections because if you don't, you just may become a victim of the Democrat's new IRS-CID "wealth-squad" attacks, even if you are not wealthy. No warning – only a sealed search warrant based on lies or innuendo from your neighbors or business competitors or corrupt informants – a sealed warrant that will take you months or years to unseal. Don't think that it can happen to you?

It happened to Senator Ted Stevens, the longest serving Republican Senator in the United States Senate. It happened to Michael Cohen, the President's own attorney. If the Government can raid a Senator's house without probable cause, how can you possibly be safe? The Attorney General was so shocked by the egregious prosecutorial misconduct against Senator Stevens that he made a motion to have all charges against him dropped. But the misconduct by the Government destroyed Senator Stevens' reputation, career and also his life. Senator Stevens, a great American, died of a broken heart in disgrace, with no chance to clear his name. You are probably not a Senator though, and neither is your wife.

You are a hard-working businessman that has applied for financial aid for your college-bound children. Your wife is a homemaker and mother of six, and you live in a middle-class neighborhood in Fort Wayne, Indiana. You do not live in Beverly Hills or in a New York City penthouse – there is absolutely nothing about your lifestyle that would lead anyone to believe you are fudging on your taxes or living beyond your means. But, even if you were cheating on your taxes, why did you not receive an audit notice? What was the reason for the armed commando raid on an innocent housewife and her daughter? Armed commando raids like this were meant to be stopped by the Roth Hearings, the Webster Commission Task Force, and the passage of the IRS Restructuring and Reform Act of 1998.

Attending the Roth Hearings on IRS abuse of the American Taxpayer, deceased New York Democratic Senator Daniel Moynihan was heard to say, "My God, we must stop these armed commando raids on American citizens." Congress did pass the necessary legislation to protect American citizens, and the Webster Commission Task Force was established to review whether the IRS-CID commandos were following the rules that the IRS had imposed on them. When the Government was sued years later in one particular Bivens Action, the IRS-CID agents testified that they could not even remember what the alleged "probable cause" was that required the armed commando raid in the first place; rather than serving an administrative audit summons, subpoena, or even a search warrant in the "least intrusive means possible." (See IRS Manual Part 9.4.6.1). (A "Bivens" Action is named after and refers to a Supreme Court case, Bivens v. Six Unknown Federal Agents, 403 U.S. 388 (1971), which allows for a civil tort claim against the Government and/or Government officials for violations of the Constitutional rights of citizens during one of these raids).

Do you expect the Courts to help save you? Forget about it. In all of those thousand-page bills that Congress passed without reading, they put in provisions that allow the IRS to assess $200,000 penalties that can grow to over a Million Dollars. These penalties are not subject to any judicial review and can be imposed by any out-of-control Field Agent of the IRS. But if you want to sue the Government, it is a very difficult thing to do. This is true even though the Supreme Court has taken away "qualified immunity" from the IRS commandos who do not follow the rules (see the IRS Manual Part 9). But in several hundred Bivens-type Actions brought against the IRS commandos to date, none were successful because the Courts always felt the "IRS must be right" or would say "I just cannot bring myself to find bad faith on the part of the Government."

As if that is not bad enough, once the innocent victims bring an action against the Government, the Government in turn then brings an action against them, tells the jury that this person committed tax fraud, and a totally innocent person spends four years in jail. If you don't believe it, see the case of Dr. Daniel Levito in which even Judge – now Supreme Court Justice – Alito states that Dr. Levito was clearly a victim of a violation of the Fourth Amendment during a commando raid of his small veterinary clinic where the Agents sent away clients of the firm, sent the employees home, and ransacked his clinic. Because Dr. Levito had the gall to sue the Government, years later he would be indicted for tax evasion and his wife was given probation for testifying against her own husband because he was exercising his First Amendment rights in advocating a book on tax avoidance. It seems only fair – since the Government put him out of business as a veterinarian – that Dr. Levito became an anti-Government, anti-tax advocate. Some of the arguments that Dr. Levito and his partners make in "their" book are totally frivolous and the IRS now has a portion of their website dedicated to these "frivolous" (if not borderline illegal) tax evasion ideas.

The protections for the American Taxpayer are also found on the IRS's own website and in the IRS's own Manual, which is available online. The Webster Commission Report is available in PDF format online. Remember, William Webster was a former Judge and the head of the CIA, and even he was shocked by the level of Government abuse of innocent American taxpayers by the IRS-CID. One of the reasons for writing this Book is that we are genuinely frightened that the new Democratic administration will want to hire even more new Special Agents who will engage in sealed search warrant, secret, armed commando raids on innocent American citizens and businesses. We use the word "innocent" because in 90% of the armed commando raids, there was no later assessment of taxes. After a two-year investigation following the raids that disrupted the business, there is no "crime" or even tax deficiency found that would have warranted the raid in the first place.

Remember, this is the IRS-CID, not the FBI or Drug Enforcement Agency or Bureau of Alcohol, Tobacco & Firearms. So, instead of serving an audit summons or subpoena, they have several dozen armed commandos in Kevlar vests with IRS-CID printed on the front, executing a sealed search warrant that you will not see for several months to several years after you file a Rule 41(g) motion in order to get your property back and unseal the warrant and affidavit.

Did we mention that President Obama tried to hire 16,000 new Special Agents for the IRS-CID just to do this sort of work? The Government only hired 800 new SEC Agents to keep Wall Street in line. This, even after the Bernie Madoff debacle and Goldman Sachs paying a fine of only a half-billion dollars for helping to bring down the economies of the Western World with toxic mortgages. Notice that friends of Goldman convinced the Government in 2009 to put in $200 billion to save AIG with $60 billion going directly to the coffers of Goldman Sachs from the

AIG guarantee of bad mortgage bonds. Lehman Brothers was allowed to go under, while AIG was saved by the Government so it could make good on the guarantees that Goldman Sachs had hoped to exploit in creating the toxic subprime mortgage market in the first place. Goldman has not had to plead guilty to anything or even admit fault.

The $550 Million fine that Goldman Sachs was forced to pay is about two weeks of revenue for Goldman – a mere traffic ticket – relatively speaking. But the same Government that will fine doctors and other small businesses up to $800,000 for failing to report a "listed" or "reportable" transaction that they did not even know they had participated in, and this is four to five years after the small business had simply adopted an ordinary pension plan with life insurance in it, lets big Wall Street firms off the hook so that they can pay record bonuses to their executives two years in a row after allegedly the greatest financial crisis since the Depression.

Of course, you cannot believe it, because you think this is America, and excessive penalties like that would violate the "excessive fines" clause of the Eighth Amendment, the "takings" clause of the Fifth Amendment, and even the "ex post facto" clause of the Constitution, because fines of this magnitude are clearly "punishments" and not traffic fines or ordinary civil penalties. But these "punishments" are meted out every day to small, unsuspecting businesses that do not have $1,000 an hour tax attorneys to defend them as does Wall Street.

The America that you grew up in is rapidly vanishing and being subsumed by an overly-intrusive Government whose uncontrolled spending is threatening your family's future financial prosperity, freedom, and in certain cases – your life. The $35 Trillion current deficit and $150 Trillion in unfunded future liabilities will either be handled by bankrupting America now or from the tears and loss of freedom by your children and grandchildren. The deficit will not go away by itself and President Biden tried to hire large numbers of new IRS-CID Special Agents who would break the law with armed commando raids into the homes and businesses of innocent American citizens. Nothing like this has happened in this Country since British troops would routinely break into the homes of Boston housewives while their husbands were at work in order to demand money to pay for an out of touch, out of control, and overly intrusive Government in England.

Make no mistake: no one in Washington cares about you. If they would raid a United States Senator's home or the homes of a former President and his campaign managers, indict them on totally bogus charges, and find them guilty through egregious prosecutorial misconduct, then you have no hope of being safe. Instead of passing the Dodd-Franks banking reform bill, Congress could have instead reinstated the Glass-Steagall Act, which served us well for 70 years. The same is true with the "up-tick rule" to stop the relentless shorting of stock by greedy and well- connected Hedge Funds, almost all of whom have accounts or friends at Goldman Sachs.

You, unfortunately, probably do not have a clue as to what we are talking about, or how this will negatively affect your future, because no one from the Government has pointed out to you all of the terrible things hidden in all of these thousand-page legislative acts that no one read. Even at this late date, you ask your candidate for the Presidency, the Senate or Congress how they feel about abortion, the death penalty, gay marriage, or gun control issues (issues which members of Congress could not possibly control even if they wanted to). Washington is squandering your resources and the Nation's resources at an unprecedented rate. You must vote Republican in this election so America can return to its greatest years of 1994-2000 when we had an intelligent and charismatic progressive President in the White House and a Republican Congress filled with deficit-hawks that did not care what anyone did behind closed doors. The Government is out of control and is dangerously close to being willing to sacrifice the future liberty and prosperity of its citizens on an altar of ever-growing deficits to fund an overly intrusive and invasive Government.

The family in Fort Wayne was not so lucky, however, and that is one of the reasons why we are writing this Book. Jim and Denise Simon of Fort Wayne, Indiana received absolutely no warning that they were under investigation by the IRS or the IRS-CID. The agent in charge of the case, Special Agent Paul Muschell, wrote an affidavit to secure the sealed search warrant that has been described by professionals to be replete with numerous factual and legal errors, clear misrepresentations of both fact and law. Testimony by Special Agent Muschell appeared to the attorneys involved in the case to be designed to mislead the magistrate judge into granting the search warrant and to have it sealed in violation of the American citizens' Fourth Amendment rights against unreasonable search and seizure. Neither Jim nor Denise Simon ever had any problems with the IRS in the past, and to this day, there has been no evidence presented that at the time of the illegal raid on the Simon's residence in Fort Wayne, Indiana, that Jim Simon had filed any false or even incorrect tax returns concerning his business affairs.

Not only was there no probable cause for the search warrant or to have the search warrant sealed, there was absolutely no reason for the raid. Does an armed commando raid of two dozen husky Special Agents with weapons drawn, covered with bulletproof vests, shouting "IRS-CID" at a housewife and her 10-year-old daughter make any sense to you? Please remember that the IRS, in its own Manual, instructs and requires the IRS-CID officer in charge to use the "least intrusive means" of investigation available in all cases (see IRM Part 9.4.6.7.3.3). When the storm troopers broke into the house of an American housewife – a mother of six – getting her youngest daughter ready for school, they accused her and her husband (who was overseas on business) with a multitude of crimes including tax evasion, fraud, money laundering, as well as other things that Denise Simon had no comprehension of and clearly did not believe or understand.

The reason this is so painfully apparent is that within a few days of the raid, Denise took her own life as she was terrified by what had transpired in her family home. The suicide letters she left to each of her six children and her husband are heart-breaking and can be found at www.rememberdenise.org. We will only reprint here the general letter she left behind proclaiming her innocence, as well as her husband's innocence, of any and all crimes of which they were accused:

> *I am truly innocent of any attempt to evade taxes, launder money, commit fraud, or any of the other things I am being accused of. I know of no attempt on Jim's part to willingly or knowingly evade taxes, launder money, commit fraud, or any of the other things he is being accused of. However, I also have no faith in the legal system or the ability of the government to seek truth. I am currently a danger to my children. I am bringing armed officers into their home. I am compelled to distance myself from them for their safety. Being innocent is simply not enough for the government. With my dying breath, I swear Jim & I are innocent.*
>
> *– Denise Simon*

As one might expect, Mr. Simon's attorneys filed all sorts of motions under the Freedom of Information Act (FOIA) to find out what this was all about. His attorneys also filed several motions to unseal the sealed search warrant affidavit submitted by Special Agent Muschell. Surprisingly, once the Court unsealed the affidavit, there was no information there to let anyone know what the Simons were actually accused of, what crimes they had allegedly committed, or why some unarmed IRS agent in a suit and a tie could not have served the Simons by mail or even better, sent a Third Party Summons to the banks where the IRS thought the Simons were hiding money. But no, the IRS-CID Special Agent involved felt that the right thing to do was to make material misrepresentations to a magistrate judge so he would sign a sealed search warrant that would "legally" allow this armed commando raid on a defenseless American housewife and her youngest daughter.

Denise admitted in her suicide notes "that she was terrified of the Government" and "she was not strong enough to fight." Despite protesting her and her husband's innocence, she admitted, "I just don't have any faith in the legal system, and I can't fight this." And that by fighting, "I can only bring danger to my family now." Where are the beers in the Rose Garden for Jim Simon and his family? Where was the Attorney General's outrage? Unfortunately for both Jim and Denise Simon, they are both white, middle class, hardworking Americans, so there is no question that this terrible incident was not motivated by race or sexual orientation, which seem to be the only issues that interest the Justice Department these days – unless they involve marijuana legalization in California or illegal immigration in Arizona. Protection of the American taxpayer's Constitutional rights in Indiana or Minnesota is not even on their radar screen.

Denise Simon is dead and she was killed by an IRS-CID Special Agent, just as if he had actually pulled the trigger. The lawsuit against the Special Agent was dismissed in 2015 under President Obama. The IRS Restructuring and Reform Act of 1998 and the Webster Commission Task Force of 1999 were meant to end these armed commando raids on unarmed and totally innocent American citizens. The "cowboys" out there like the IRS Agents need to be stopped and brought to justice before their lies to magistrate judges kill someone else. But if the President will not protect you, and the Attorney General and the Department of Justice will not protect you, who can you trust to help you? Well, that brings us full circle as to why you need to vote in this upcoming election.

The same Congressman and Senator that is powerless to help you regulate abortion, the death penalty, gay marriage, or guns and drugs in the streets, is exactly the person who can vote to curtail the monstrous, illegal and unconstitutional activities of the IRS. Only Congress can stop that. If you vote for Kamala Harris and vote for the Democrat Senator or Congressman this November, you can be sure that your food, energy, and healthcare bills will all be much more expensive, your taxes higher, your freedoms taken away and the future a lot less bright than it could have been – and should have been if we followed the Constitution. Regardless of who is to blame for the current state of affairs, your future financial security, freedom, and even your life are on the line this time, this election.

The wealthy know how to avoid taxes. The big corporations all incorporate offshore companies, and legally pay no taxes. So why do the Special Agents of the IRS-CID pick on people like Denise and Jim Simon? **Because they can**. You do not see IRS-CID Special Agents planning an IRS-CID raid on Goldman Sachs, and the abuse by IRS Agents will not be stopped by President Harris, a Democratic Attorney General, Treasury Secretary, or the Department of Justice. It is only when the IRS is made to account for its actions in front of a Republican President and a Republican Congress that you will be safe from unauthorized Government intrusions into your affairs and your homes due to the misguided intentions of the Obama and Biden Administrations and their progeny. This Book was written to help you and your family, and we pray that we are not too late.

Chapter Ten
IN ORDER TO FORM A MORE PERFECT UNION

"Be thankful that we are not getting all the government that we are paying for".

- Will Rogers

Where is my $10,000,000 loan?

Recently a former regulator in the Government bemoaned the fact that Trillions of dollars were wasted in the most anemic, if not totally stalled, recovery since the Great Recession of 2008-2009. She made the modest proposal that it would have been better to have the Federal Reserve lend $10,000,000 to each American family rather than all of the Billions and Trillions that were lent to the banks at near zero percent interest rates. Her point was that the most conservative families could invest in ten-year Treasury bonds, as the banks are doing, and earn a conservative and guaranteed four percent or $400,000 return per year. With every American family earning $400,000 per year, the recession-depression would be over. There would be no need to have 700,000 Americans declare bankruptcy each year because they could not pay their medical bills. Middle class parents would have money to put their children through college without going deeper in debt, and the next generation would not have $100,000 of student loans hanging around their neck like an anchor. With $400,000 per year, per family, no one would need to be foreclosed out of their home, and if someone "walked" on their mortgage, there would be a dozen young families ready to step in to buy the house rather than paying non-deductible rent on a small apartment.

There would also be plenty of money to pay bloated health insurance premiums caused by President Obama's Affordable Care Act. The "Affordable Care" Act will become the greatest example of Orwellian "Doublespeak" in the Twenty-First Century. The so- called "free-riders" who went to emergency rooms because they did not have health insurance cost American hospitals – and the American public – about $16 Billion a year. Now the new Democratic Health Plan according to the non-partisan Congressional Budget Office (CBO) will cost America as much as Two Trillion Dollars, or more than 100 times the current amount, over a ten-year period. The CBO has a wonderful website that should be required reading for all American citizens. Along with the Government Accountability Office (GAO), there are a number of Government agencies that provide excellent reports and studies, are well run, and save the Government more than they cost the taxpayer because the analysis they do is so thorough and comprehensive. These websites give you a realistic, non-political view of the State of the Union, and the state of the Union is not good. In fact, its situation is dire, critical, and on life support.

For example, from those websites you can learn that in the President's time in office, American families have lost a staggering amount of family wealth, and we are now at the 1992 average family wealth or at the time of President George H.W. Bush or Bush (41).

You could also learn from the Government websites that the Treasury Inspector General, The Honorable J. Russell George, has discovered that the IRS has distributed almost SIX BILLION DOLLARS in fraudulent tax refunds – several thousand of which went to the same address in Michigan – and if this identify theft and tax fraud is not stopped immediately, the IRS's negligence will cost the American taxpayers more than TWENTY BILLION DOLLARS over the next five years. Therefore, according to a report from the Government and Treasury Inspector General George – a report that is available on the Internet – the IRS's inability to stop tax-refund fraud is actually a larger problem than lower income people going to hospital emergency rooms without insurance.

Not only did America lose its benchmark "AAA" status last year, average income and median income for working families has gone down over the past ten years. The percentage of Americans who are able to work, but cannot find work, is at an all-time low – nearly 61%.

Forget the often-unreliable unemployment rates published monthly, because many people have either not applied for unemployment benefits or stopped looking for work altogether. Moreover, disability payments have soared as a new form of "unemployment" compensation.

The only thing that has steadily gone up is the poverty rate, which, at over 15% is the highest it has been since the war on poverty began in 1963. Just like the war on drugs, it appears that "Poverty" has won the war – with 50,000,000 Americans now living below the poverty level, with no health insurance, and without opportunity or hope.

This year, for the first time in history, the wealth of the average Canadian family has actually surpassed the wealth of the average American family. Obviously, we need the Keystone Pipeline more than the Canadians need us and fairly soon, the Canadians will close their borders to us, their poor neighbors to the South. Senior citizens will need to sneak across both borders to get the prescription drugs they need at a price they can afford. A good example is the notorious Boston criminal Whitey Bulger who, while hiding from the Government in California for his murders and crimes in Boston, was able to regularly cross the border into Mexico to get his prescription drugs.

So, pretend this book is written for you. Pretend it is the Christmas season of 1776. America is about to be born. You are poor, hungry, cold, sick and sleeping outdoors in the cold and wind. You are here to fight and die for your family's future. The Government does not care about you and answers only to the aristocracy and the plutocratic elites that really run the Country. Today, everything is great for the people at the top – and the people at the top rig the game by utilizing the Federal Reserve, the big banks, and even Wall Street itself so they can keep winning at your expense. And if they lose every once in a while, they turn their private speculation into massive public debt under the theory that they are "too big to fail."

The plutocrats and the aristocrats control the Democratic Party and all branches of the Government. If you really want to change things, you must stand up for yourself and think for yourself.

As a citizen during the revolution, you will read tonight by the campfire "The American Crisis" by Thomas Paine, and in the early morning while everyone is asleep – we will cross the river together to fight for the new America and leave the old one behind. If you believe in freedom, if you believe in helping your family have a better future, and if you believe that the government that governs least, governs best, it is time to join a new movement.

Let us start a new revolution to make America the country that it was meant to be. Let us work together to "form a more perfect union" and STOP those who would destroy the America that the Founders and Patriots dreamed of on that Christmas Eve so many years ago, when they fought and died to protect your Declaration of Independence. You owe it to them, and you owe it to your family and future family to do what you can to make America the promised land that it was always meant to be. We are waiting for you to join us and join "The Plot to Save America" before it is too late.

Chapter Eleven
THE DECLARATION OF ENERGY INDEPENDENCE

"It is dangerous to be Right, when the Government is Wrong"

- Voltaire

America's energy crisis is a self-inflicted wound. We overtax our fellow Americans by Trillions of dollars to fund needless wars fought in desert territories where the locals despise us and where we cannot trust our supposed allies to lift a finger to help us.

But right now, there is a glut of natural gas in America, and it has been determined that we have 300 years' worth of natural gas just in America. Don't worry, a discussion of drilling in Alaska is coming up next, but if we are the "Saudi Arabia" of natural gas, why are we not converting everyone's oil burners to natural gas, and why not convert all utilities to natural gas or nuclear power? Why not have all Government vehicles, all city buses, and all large trucks required to run on liquefied natural gas? Saudi Arabia has publicly acknowledged that they must keep the price of oil above $90 per barrel to pay for all of the public welfare programs that they have promised their people. But in America, because of the current glut of natural gas, the price has plummeted from the high seven-dollar range to below the two-dollar range in some cases.

Forget wind and everything else, why wouldn't the President support natural gas drilling everywhere, the Keystone project, and any other American natural gas drilling projects? As far as our trading partners are concerned, the President's "actions" speak much louder than his words.

If the Democrats were truly serious about allowing increased drilling in America, it would not have cost Shell Oil over FOUR BILLION DOLLARS just for EPA approvals and environmental studies to drill offshore from Prudhoe Bay, Alaska, which has been the most successful source of oil production in North America. No one pays income taxes in Alaska, except for the "seven sisters" oil companies. Instead, each Alaska citizen receives an annual dividend distribution from the Permanent Fund that is a multi-billion-dollar fund created by the drilling from Prudhoe Bay.

Moreover, the Alaska Pipeline created hundreds of Millions of dollars in jobs and incomes for young people from all over America that flocked to Alaska, just as Americans now flock to North Dakota for jobs or could have flocked to the Keystone project had the President not scuttled the building of the new pipeline to let energy flow from the oil sands of Canada to the refineries in Oklahoma and Louisiana.

Drilling just in the areas where we know there are great treasure troves of oil can turn the tables on OPEC and change our energy dependence into energy independence. If only the American people understood the great wealth lying underground and underwater in Alaska, while Millions in America go cold in the winter and stay at home in the Summer because of the price of oil.

So why have the great Alaskan oil reserves not been tapped? Environmentalists have run out of logical excuses, and if the President and members of Congress cared more about the American people and less about the migration and mating habits of the caribou, the drilling would have already started in the Arctic National Wildlife Refuge in (ANWR) and the National Petroleum Reserve in Alaska (NPRA). The Alaskan people – and especially the Alaskan Native Communities – all favor drilling in Alaska. Even the caribou love to make homes near the Alaskan Pipeline to keep warm. But it is the American people in the lower 48 states that are ignorant of the immense size of Alaska, the relatively microscopic size of the typical drilling site, and the incredible wealth that ordinary Americans could enjoy from the renewed drilling in Alaska.

To understand the immense size of Alaska, imagine if you could pick up Alaska from an old flat Mercator map of the World. If you placed Alaska and its islands over the Continental United States, it would stretch from California to South Carolina and take up virtually the entire lower 48 states. If you cut out from your imaginary map California, Texas and Florida, Alaska could cover the entire Continental United States, as Alaska covers 425,000,000 acres of land.

The regions that we are talking about drilling in ANWR and

NPRA have 19,287,000 acres and 23,500,000 acres, respectively. Yet, certain people in Washington, D.C. would rather spend Trillions in fighting needless wars in Kuwait, Iraq and Iran to protect the Straits of Hormuz for the Saudis, rather than open up the tremendous wealth of Alaska to protect what – the caribou?

As it stands now, Prudhoe Bay has about 1,100 oil wells on 213,500 acres. The fighting is all about opening another 2,200 acres for drilling. Downtown Houston is only about 1,200 acres and has just one oil company, a small oil company, Callon Petroleum which is developing the 8,800 acres that it owns in the Texas range known as the Permian Basin. The Permian Basin in Texas is approximately 240,000 square miles (800 miles by 300 miles), which means that it is 153,600,000 acres, at 640 acres per square mile. Therefore, just the Texan Permian Basin is larger than the entire state of Oklahoma, and twice the size of New England.

The site in ANWR that oil companies would like to open up for new drilling is only about 2,200 acres out of 19,000,000 acres in ANWR, and 425,000,000 acres in Alaska. As a point of reference, the Ted Stevens International Airport in Anchorage is about double that space, at 4,800 acres. Arguably, no one in Washington, D.C. would care if the Anchorage Airport doubled in size to 9,600 acres – so why the fight to prevent drilling in ANWR or new drilling in Prudhoe Bay or off the coast of Barrow?

So now that you are imagining that Alaska is bigger than the Continental United States minus Texas, California, and a few other outlying states; and that the famous fertile oil ground of the Permian Basin in Texas is actually larger than the State of Oklahoma; let us consider Death Valley National Park in California. Death Valley grew by 1,200,000 acres to a total of 3,336,000 acres and was designated a national park with the passage of the Desert Protection Act of October 31, 1994. But of the 3,336,000 acres in Death Valley National Park, well over 3,000,000 acres is pure, undeveloped desert wilderness. There is nothing at all in the 3,000,000 acres of desert wilderness, and what people think of the actual park itself that tourists go to is a much smaller area.

Is there any doubt that if gold or oil was discovered on the Death Valley property that it would have been developed – or mined – rather than be left as desert? For an answer to that question, one need only look at upper class neighborhoods in California, like Huntington Beach, that have small active oil wells all over town.

Now, assume that oil was discovered in Death Valley, enough to transform the California economy from its near-bankrupt state to a wealthy oil producer the size of Norway or Venezuela, and worthy of OPEC membership. Imagine that you can get all of the oil that you want from the 300,000 acres that are already somewhat developed and you will leave untouched the 3,000,000 acres of pristine desert wilderness. How would you vote? Now, how would you feel if some East Coast senators from small states were blocking your state from financial surplus and full employment? Remember, in Alaska there is no income tax or sales tax. There are only royalty payments by the big oil companies to the Permanent Fund for the citizens of Alaska to receive annual dividends.

What if we just thought of the property that has been abandoned by the Government in the Continental United States, known as "Brownfields?" The Government Accountability Office (GAO) estimates that there are approximately 425,000 Brownfield sites throughout the United States.

"Brownfields" are industrial sites that have some sort of environmental pollutant problem or chemical hazard such as oil, paint, or other dangerous chemicals that makes the land toxic or unusable. The GAO estimates that there are over 5,000,000 acres of abandoned industrial sites just in our nation's cities. This is roughly the same amount of land occupied by our 60 largest cities. Remember, downtown Houston is just about 1,800 acres. This is land that we have voluntarily abandoned and refuse to use or develop for anything.

As part of the Brownfields reclamation project, the Government can require that the abandoned sites that receive Government grants for cleaning up the sites use the money to facilitate the building of new energy sources, including green energy and alternative fuels. For example, an abandoned Army base in Arizona or Nevada can have acres and acres of solar panels and wind turbines to create new sources of power for the surrounding communities. Even if not competitive at first, over a period of three to five years, the projects will pay for themselves, and then the next twenty years the project will be producing abundant amounts of low cost, clean, and renewable energy from abandoned environmental waste sites.

America already has 5,000,000 acres of abandoned land that no one is trying to reclaim or save. New oil wells in just 2,000 acres of ANWR can help to end our energy dependence on countries that are actually hostile to us.

As mentioned above, the famous drilling spot in Alaska, Prudhoe Bay, on the North Slope, has 1,100 wells on 213,500 acres. We are willing to leave 3,000,000 acres undisturbed in Death Valley. Arguably, the most beautiful – and the most famous of the National Parks – Yellowstone National Park, has only 2,219,789 acres in total. I say "only" because we could carve eight or nine "Yellowstones" out of ANWR and NPRA to keep as "wilderness" and no one would notice the land we opened up for drilling. We only foresee 200,000 acres for drilling in each of the Alaskan preserves and no one would miss the land or even see the oil wells from any of the new "national parks" established in ANWR or NPRA. And remember the current fight is over only 2,200-2,500 acres for drilling. Also, please remember that NPRA stands for National Petroleum Reserve in Alaska. What are we waiting for?

It is also important to note that Yellowstone Park is bigger than several East Coast states, including Delaware and Rhode Island combined. In 1988, wildfires destroyed over 800,000 acres of Yellowstone, or an area the size of Rhode Island at 793,880 acres. So, if Mother Nature could destroy 800,000 acres of one of our most beautiful National Parks without Congressional action, and we have already abandoned 5,000,000 acres of Brownfields, then why would Congress not answer the prayers of all Alaskans, and most Americans, to just open up 200,000 acres in each of ANWR and NPRA for oil drilling? After all, the National Petroleum Reserve was originally called the Naval Petroleum Reserve in Alaska to save a large source of oil for future American warships. If not now, then when?

Every day we hear people in Government and pundits on air saying that we should open up the American Strategic Petroleum Reserve, which really was meant for emergencies like another oil embargo as happened in the 1970s, not to regulate the price of oil against hedge funds, speculators, and the Arab states in OPEC. The President could end oil speculation tomorrow by stopping the purchase of oil on margin. As previously mentioned above, just look at the price of silver in 2011 after margin requirements were increased, not once but twice. Silver is just a metal for jewelry and coinage. Oil is the lifeblood of the American economy, and the President should end the market for speculators the day after he reads this book; and before releasing any oil from the American Strategic Petroleum Reserve, allow

Shell to start drilling off Prudhoe Bay in Barrow, Alaska, and open up only 1% of ANWR and NPRA to drilling, and approve the Keystone Pipeline project.

Just as Congress has decided to auction off the airwaves to increase broadband capabilities and add to the public coffers, drilling can be opened up on national lands by having oil companies and entrepreneurs bid for the drilling rights by agreeing to pay a royalty to a Federal trust fund that would benefit all Americans, as the Alaskan Permanent Fund benefits all Alaskans.

The oil companies and new oil entrepreneurs would still pay taxes – as would the Million-plus newly hired oil company employees that would be hired to work on the new oil drilling projects in Alaska and elsewhere. Cut the Washington, D.C. bureaucracy, red tape, and overly-zealous regulations and create a new Permanent Fund for all Americans. Imagine the North Dakota Bakken Shale project, and multiply it by 25 times for the amount of oil in ANWR and NPRA.

With all of the excitement about the Canadian oil sands project and the Keystone Pipeline; ANWR, NPRA, and Alaskan off-shore drilling, which is all American, dwarfs any other North American project by a large multiple. Combined with the 300 years of natural gas that America has, and all of the other alternative energy options discussed in this book, the President only has himself to blame if a barrel of oil ever goes over $100 again.

When the President took office in January 2009, gasoline was at an average of $1.85 per gallon. In February 2012, gasoline has more than doubled to over $3.90 a gallon. This does not include state or federal taxes which make the cost of gasoline to the consumer between $4.00 to $4.50 a gallon; with premium gas hitting close to $5.00 a gallon in several areas, and by the Summer, perhaps gasoline will be $5.00 per gallon across the country unless, of course, the country falls back into recession.

The NPRA has 23,500,000 acres, or roughly the size of Maine (22,646,400 acres), and ANWR has 19,287,000 acres, which equals the rest of New England combined (NH, VT, MA, CT, RI). Barrow, Alaska is smaller in acreage – and population – than Bridgeport, Connecticut. But who would not choose to revitalize both Bridgeport and all of Connecticut (currently ranked 50th of all states in job production and job growth, as well as near the bottom of states to retire to) by allowing drilling in and surrounding Bridgeport?

There is, of course, no prospect for that happening even in the distant future, but that is not the point. No one has discovered oil in or near Bridgeport. But North Dakota has 45,248,000 acres and currently sports the lowest unemployment in the nation, a state budget in surplus, very low taxes, and prosperity everywhere because the Bakken Shale Oil Field has 6,000 active wells on only 900,000 acres. South Dakota, which has 48,000,000 acres, has several oil discoveries, all of which are smaller than the 244,000 acres marked off as the Badlands National Park. Suffice it to say, North and South Dakota have already made the decision that they will take whatever steps necessary to develop state and private lands to secure the future prosperity of their individual states.

No one in North Dakota is saying to suspend the North Dakota "payroll" or unemployment tax to allow people from North Dakota to afford the ever-increasing cost of gasoline. Once again, to put things in prospective, Prudhoe Bay, surrounding the small town of Barrow, Alaska, has only 1,100 wells on 215,000 acres, but it produces about 480,000 barrels per day and is running down. The Bakken Shale Oil Field has over 6,000 wells and is just getting started.

Similarly, while Alaska is a very large area, it only has a population of about 700,000 people. Kuwait, on the other hand, is only 11,000 square miles, where the Permian Basin in Texas is over 240,000 square miles. Kuwait has a population of 2,000,000 people, but 60% of that population is comprised of foreigners who work on the oil fields and other oil-related or menial jobs to support the ruling class. But Kuwait, as an oil-producing nation, only produces 2,000,000 barrels per day – only four times the daily production of Prudhoe Bay. While Kuwait's production accounts for only 3% of the World's output, the oil production for Kuwait and Saudi Arabia combined account for an impressive 80% of the World's excess production. The more a nation has of "excess production," the more it can export.

By opening ANWR and NPRA to drilling, Alaska can match the daily production of Kuwait, and more. In 1998, the Bureau of Land Management proposed to open up drilling and sell new leases for Alaska's North Slope Borough. The proposal was to open only 600,000 acres of the neighboring 50,000,000 acres. Prudhoe Bay is already there, as is Barrow, Alaska.

Inexplicably, the Bush (43) Administration decided in June of 2005 to block the sale of the leases for no good reason. This is indeed ironic in that we have wasted more than a Trillion dollars in a needless war in Iraq, which was supposedly over oil or weapons of mass destruction. The original Iraq war, based on Iraq's invasion of Kuwait under Bush (41), cost $68 Billion, but most of this was reimbursed by willing partners that wanted Kuwait's excess production to keep flowing to Europe and the West. Almost no one supported us in Bush (43)'s fiasco in Iraq, much less reimbursed us for our trillion-dollar folly in the desert.

No more tax subsidies for electric golf carts or windmills or Government boondoggles like Solyndra. Let's stop "crucifying" the oil companies and let them have the 2,200 acres in ANWR and expand the current offshore drilling in Prudhoe Bay.

Chapter Twelve
FOURTEEN POUNDS OF SUGAR

"The country has to awaken every now and then to   the fact that the people are responsible for the government they get. And when they elect a man to the presidency who doesn't take care of the job, they've got nobody to blame but themselves."

- Harry Truman

The original title of this chapter was going to be "Fuel at Forty Cents a Gallon," but then no one would read it as being total science fiction. Truly wise and informed individuals can already guess what this chapter is all about, but what everyone in the United States, from the President on down, should understand is that it takes just fourteen pounds of sugar to make a gallon of sugar-based ethanol fuel. Forget about corn- based ethanol, which is too expensive, and forget about sugar in your local grocery store that is kept at 20 cents a pound because of government tariffs and sugar cartel pricing, and instead think about inedible sugar at two cents a pound. It takes 14 pounds of sugar, plus water, plus yeast to make a gallon of sugar-based ethanol that can run just fine in most modern cars.

Everyone now realizes that "corn-based" ethanol subsidies provided to make corn-based alternative sources of energy has been an expensive failure, for the government and the public. Corn-based ethanol greatly inflates the price of corn whether for corn flakes, food for cattle and pigs (and therefore meat products all go up in price), and even corn-based syrups and sweeteners (that makes soft drinks and snacks go up in price).

As former New York Mayor and billionaire Michael Bloomberg has made clear, sugar is a killer. It is bad for humans to consume, even worse for your health than smoking. All of the hidden sugar in the American diet leads to obesity, diabetes, "diabesity," and even Alzheimer's and Dementia are being referred to by doctors as Type III Diabetes. Thirty years ago — none of the fifty states had an obesity problem. Now, all fifty states have obesity healthcare cases in epidemic proportions. There are no less than two dozen films available on Netflix streaming that show the problems of sugar in the American diet. It seems that PBS public television has a special every Sunday by some notable doctor talking about how deadly sugar in the American diet is to the average American. Both the New York Times Magazine and 60 Minutes have had cover stories on the dangers of sugar. We are literally killing our children as well as ourselves. But that is for another book, another day.

The incredible, fantastic, unbelievably "good" sugar is inedible sugar, that we can get from Mexico at two cents a pound or from our new free-trade partner Colombia at one cent a pound. But even at two cents a pound, that would be $40 per ton of inedible sugar. Each ton of inedible sugar at $40 per ton could produce 140 gallons of sugar-based ethanol. It would take more than three barrels of oil at $70 per barrel for West Texas Intermediate or at

$75 per barrel for Brent Crude to produce the same amount of energy.

There is no question that you would not use sugar- based ethanol in a high-performance, high- octane car like a Maserati, but how many average Americans have a Maserati? Instead, most ordinary automobiles manufactured after 1990 can be retro-fitted with a device that costs about $120 and you just need a friendly teenager/ gearhead or a local service station to install the device for you, and it will allow your car to accept sugar-based fuel as well as regular gasoline.

In most states, you can build an in-house "still" for yourself to distill spirits and get a permit for free, as long as you are not selling drinkable alcohol and you are making less than 50 gallons a day. Obviously, the sugar- based fuel is for your car and is not fit for human consumption. You should, and we do, put a "skull and crossbones" on the container, and keep it away from children. Do not store it; just put it in your gas tank.

If you Google "making your own still" or "creating sugar-based ethanol," you will find several offers for directions on how to make your own still for between $39 and $79. Many people who make in-home wine or beer already understand that just by adding sugar to water plus some yeast will create the alcoholic mash. You then take that mash to begin the distilling process, which just evaporates the "water" from the "alcohol" mix to produce the 90% pure alcohol.

If there is one industry that goes back to the beginning days of the Republic, it is how to make "moonshine" or "white-lightning" or "bathtub" gin. Whatever your poison of preference, Americans have been making alcohol, liquor, and booze longer and better than anyone including the French and Italians. Remember, wine poured in your car will just ruin the engine, but authentic and pure Kentucky or Tennessee "moonshine" can power it.

Even our first President, George Washington, had five stills on his Virginia farm that produced 11,000-15,000 gallons of alcohol per year. Even to this day, most states will give a person a permit for free to have his own homemade still, as long as the alcohol will not be sold or distributed; and as we stated, our brand of ethanol is to be put in your car, not in your mouth.

Last year, the typical American spent over $4,200 a year on gas. Figure 1,100 gallons a year at $3.50-$3.80 per gallon, the highest annual cost in American history. That means it takes 20-25 gallons of gas to fill up the typical American car on Saturday or Sunday for the coming week, and that means $80-$100 per fill up. With sugar- based fuel, the person could distill the same 20 gallons at a cost of 40 cents per gallon and fill up the family car for eight to ten dollars a week from the family's homemade George Washington-type still.

Why is this important? Because Brazil as a nation is already energy independent and sees no reason to send troops to Iraq or

Iran to keep open the Straits of Hormuz. Brazil has an embarrassment of natural riches and can produce enough sugar-based ethanol to fuel its cars so that it can export sugar, tobacco, and oil to China to keep the Dragon well-fed and happy. Brazil spends no money to "police" the World and is actually hiring more American engineers than America is at the present time because of all of the energy projects, infrastructure, and building projects going on there. Strangely enough, Brazil has purposefully increased the cost of its sugar- based fuels to prop up its budding oil industry. Brazil has other natural resources like hydro-electric power and advanced technologies from prominent American companies like General Electric, whose reported growth in Brazil has been dramatic, if not positively phenomenal; where its growth in America has been stagnant or even non-existent.

Brazil is without a doubt a natural resources superpower; but so are we. A little-known American Government report actually states that America could grow more sugar cane more profitably than Brazil. If we add our free trade agreements with Mexico and Columbia, we can produce more sugar-based fuel than Brazil, even cheaper than Brazil can. Also, assuming relations can be normalized in the future, Cuba can once again become a sugar producing colony for America.

Imagine oil tankers crossing the Gulf of Mexico filled with tons of sugar instead of barrels of oil. No Somalian pirates, no terrorist attacks, no threats to close the Straits of Hormuz or threats by OPEC to raise prices. Imagine a renewable energy source that is abundant, cheap, clean-burning, environment-friendly and American – whether from North America or Latin America, it is still ours or in friendly hands.

But what about refining? Since the Environmental Protection Agency (EPA) was founded in the early 1970s, it has not approved a single new refinery as being clean enough and the cost to improve and update old refineries has caused many refineries to be shut down or go out of business. Entities not involved in the oil refining business – such as Delta Airlines – have been forced to buy refineries to insure a future source of jet fuel if more refineries close.

Now imagine large, clean distilleries set up in Louisiana to replace old, dirty refineries. The EPA would not oppose a new "Grey Goose" premium vodka distillery on the Bayou, whereas a new oil refinery would be dead on arrival. Even Alaska has had problems getting permission to build a refinery in Valdez at the end of the Alaskan pipeline. Currently, there is a 60 million gallon a year ethanol distillery for sale in Louisiana for less than $5,000,000. So, we could buy 100 active distilleries across the country for just one failed Solyndra? How many jobs would that create?

And add "sugar- fuel" distribution to the Wal- Mart in your town or the five liquor stores in your town – buy a case of sugar-based fuel at your local store for $5.00 to $6.00 and that will get you through the week.

There are already small machine-based sugar distilleries available for $10,000 a piece, but a personal still can be put together at a cost of $200 to $500 even with brand new parts. Junk-yard distillers can be put together by creative people at almost no cost at all. The device to make your car sugar-friendly costs a one-time $120 fee and perhaps $50 for an instruction manual or the labor to have someone install it.

Remember the Whiskey Rebellion of 1791-1794? If each small business of 15 employees in America puts together the same type of family-farm still that George Washington did for his family at a cost of $500 and purchased 15 ethanol converters for each employee's car at $120 apiece for $1,800, for a total of under $2,500 for the company independent fuel project. Giving each of the qualifying 750,000 businesses a WHISKIE (Washington Home Individual Small Business Key Initiative for Energy Independence) tax deduction of $2,000 would cost the Government approximately $600 per company in a 30% tax bracket, or roughly $450,000,000 for the entire nation to be energy independent. That is $50,000,000 less than President Obama spent on Solyndra and his cash- bundling political cronies; and now we have made 750,000 small businesses and over 20,000,000 American families energy independent from the Middle East.

Now, do we really think 750,000 small businesses are going to set up stills like George Washington did? No, of course not, but that is not the point. And there is no reason to complicate the

Tax Code with one more tax deduction or tax credit, no matter how well intentioned it may be. The point is that the technology is already available to make America energy independent, and it has been available to Americans to have a still on their family farm or in the back of the garage or the office building, just like George Washington did 260 years ago. Energy costs for a small business' employees could go from $60,000-$80,000 per year down to a few thousand per year for the whole company and their families. The water is plentiful and free and even recycled or dirty water can be used for this project because no one is drinking the fuel and the water will be evaporated during the distillation process.

We do not need tax credits or tax deductions or federal loans for the President's cronies – we just need common sense and to get other Washington bureaucratic administrators of liquor off our backs and allow free and ample permits for up to 15,000 gallons per year for non-drinkable alcohol.

Once every American individual and every small business can be energy independent, someone will become the local "distiller" of choice for the neighborhood. The best of those neighborhood distillers will become the distiller for the town; and the best of those will become the best in the county, the state and then the region. Then there will be a new John D. Rockefeller or Sam Walton of distilled energy who makes cheap fuel available to everyone across the country, wherever they may be.

Former President Obama and his Democrat Solyndra-crony

elite friends are part of the problem; they are not part of any solution. When any President says that he has "no solution or silver bullet" for the energy problems facing our nation, you should take his word for it, believe him, and then vote for someone who will at least explore the possible solutions out there, even if they are not perfect. Allowing small businesses to set up a still to produce and provide sugar-based fuel for their employees would be a good start in the right direction.

If we invest in anything as a nation, it should be in cost-effective energy solutions, delivery of those solutions, and the infrastructure to support them.

Chapter Thirteen
A PRAYER FOR AMERICA

*"For on the strength of our free economy rests
the hope of all free nations. I shall not fail that
hope — for free men and free nations must
prosper and they must prevail."*

- John F. Kennedy

America's rise to world leadership in the past century has reflected more than anything else our unprecedented economic growth. Interrupted during the decade of the 30s, the vigorous expansion of our economy resumed in 1940 and continued thereafter. It demonstrated for all to see the power of freedom and the efficiency of free institutions. The economic health of this nation has been, up until now, fundamentally sound.

But a leading nation, a nation upon which all depend, in this country and around the world, cannot afford to be satisfied, to look back, or to pause. Our strength and growth depend the strength of others, the spread of free world trade and unity, and continued confidence in our leadership and our currency. The underdeveloped countries are dependent upon us for the sale of their primary commodities and for aid to their struggling economies. In short, a prosperous and growing America is important not only to Americans, it is, as the spokesman for the Western nations in the Organization for Economic Cooperation and Development, of vital importance to the entire World.

This economy is capable of producing, without strain, much more than we are producing today. Business earnings could be seven to eight times higher than they are today. Utilization of existing plant and equipment could be much higher — and, if it were, investment would rise. We need not accept an unemployment rate of nine percent or more, such as we have had for the last 36 months. There is no need for us to be satisfied with a rate of growth that keeps good men out of work and good capacity out of use.

We are all, of course, familiar with these problems. The rate of insured unemployment has been persistently higher here than the national average, and the increases in personal income and employment have been slower here than in the nation as a whole. You have seen the tragedy of chronically depressed areas, of unemployed young people — and I think this might be one of our most serious national problems, unemployed young people, those under 20. One out of four are unemployed, particularly those in the minority groups, and others on relief at an early age with the prospect that in this decade we will have between seven and eight million school dropouts, unskilled, coming into the labor market, at a time when the need for unskilled labor is steadily diminishing. And we know you share our conviction that this nation's economy can and must do better than it has done in the last five years. Our choice, therefore, boils down to one of: doing nothing, and thereby risking a widening gap between our actual and potential growth in output, profits, and employment

— or taking action at the federal level, to raise our entire economy to a new and higher level of business activity.

If we do not take action, those who have the most reason to be dissatisfied with our present rate of growth will be tempted to seek shortsighted and narrow solutions — to resist automation, to reduce the work week to 35 hours or even lower, to shut out imports, or to raise prices in a vain effort to obtain full capacity profits on under-capacity operations. But these are all self-defeating expedients which can only restrict the economy, not expand it.

There are a number of ways by which the federal government can meet its responsibilities to aid economic growth. It can and must improve American education and technical training. It can and must expand civilian research and technology. One of the great bottlenecks for this country's economic growth in this decade will be the shortages of doctorates in mathematics, engineering, and physics — a serious shortage with a great demand and an undersupply of highly trained manpower. We can and must step up the development of our natural resources.

But the most direct and significant kind of federal action aiding economic growth is to make possible an increase in private consumption and investment demand — to cut the fetters which hold back private spending. In the past, this could be done in part by the increased use of credit and monetary tools, but our balance of payments situation today places limits on our use of those tools for expansion. It could also be done by increasing federal expenditures faster than necessary, but such a course would soon demoralize both the government and our economy.

If government is to retain the confidence of the people, it must not spend more than can be justified on grounds of national need or spent with maximum efficiency. And we shall say more on this in a moment. The final and best means of strengthening demand among consumers and business is to reduce the burden on private income and the deterrents to private initiative which are imposed by our present tax system. We are not talking about a "quickie" or a temporary tax cut, which would be more appropriate if a recession were imminent. Nor are we talking about giving the economy a mere shot in the arm, to ease some temporary complaint. We are talking about the accumulated evidence of the last five years that our present tax system, developed as it was, in good part, during World War II to restrain growth, exerts too heavy a drag on growth in peace time; that it siphons out of the private economy too large a share of personal and business purchasing power; that it reduces the financial incentives for personal effort, investment, and risk-taking.

In short, to increase demand and lift the economy, the federal government's most useful role is not to rush into a program of excessive increases in public expenditures, but to expand the incentives and opportunities for private expenditures. Under these circumstances, any new tax legislation — and you can understand that under the comity which exists in the United

States Constitution whereby the Ways and Means Committee in the House of Representatives have the responsibility of initiating this legislation, that the details of any proposal should wait on the meeting of the Congress in January. But you can understand that, under these circumstances, in general, that any new tax legislation enacted next year should meet the following three tests:

First, it should reduce the net taxes by a sufficiently early date and a sufficiently large amount to do the job required. Early action could give us extra leverage, added results, and important insurance against recession. Too large a tax cut, of course, could result in inflation and insufficient future revenues — but the greater danger is a tax cut too little, or too late, to be effective. Second, the new tax bill must increase private consumption, as well as investment. Consumers are still spending between 92 and 94 percent on their after-tax income, as they have every year since 1950. But that after-tax income could and should be greater, providing stronger markets for the products of American industry. When consumers purchase more goods, plants use more of their capacity, men are hired instead of laid-off, investment increases, and profits are high.

Corporate tax rates must also be cut to increase incentives and the availability of investment capital. The government has already taken major steps to reduce business tax liability and to stimulate the modernization, replacement, and expansion of our productive plant and equipment. Now we need to increase consumer demand to make these measures fully effective — demand which will make more use of existing capacity and thus increase both profits and the incentive to invest. In fact, profits after taxes would be at least 15 percent higher today if we were operating at full employment. For all these reasons, next year's tax legislation should reduce personal as well as corporate income taxes: for those in the lower brackets, who are certain to spend their additional take- home pay, and for those in the middle and upper brackets, who can thereby be encouraged to undertake additional efforts and enabled to invest more capital.

Third, the new tax legislation should improve both the equity and the simplicity of our present tax system. This means the enactment of long-needed tax reforms, a broadening of the tax base, and the elimination or modification of many special tax privileges. These steps are not only needed to recover lost revenue and thus make possible a larger cut in present rates, they are also tied directly to our goal of greater growth. For the present patchwork of special provisions and preferences lightens the tax loads of some only at the cost of placing a heavier burden on others. It distorts economic judgments and channels undue amounts of energy into efforts to avoid tax liability. It makes certain types of less productive activity more profitable than other more valuable undertakings. All this inhibits our growth and efficiency, as well as considerably complicating the work of both the taxpayer and the Internal Revenue Service.

These various exclusions and concessions have been justified [in the past] as a means of overcoming oppressively high rates in the upper brackets, and a sharp reduction in those rates accompanied by base- broadening, loophole-closing measures would properly make the new rates not only lower, but also more widely applicable. Surely this is more equitable on both counts. Those are the three tests which the right kind of legislation must meet — and we are confident that the enactment of the right bill next year will in due course increase our gross national product by several times the amount of taxes actually cut. Profit margins will be improved, and both the incentive to invest and the supply of internal funds for investment will be increased. There will be new interest in taking risks, in increasing productivity, in creating new jobs and new products for long-term economic growth. Other national problems, moreover, will be aided by full employment. It will encourage the location of new plants in areas of labor surplus — and provide new jobs for workers that we are retraining — and facilitate the adjustment which will be necessary under our new trade expansion bill, and reduce a number of government expenditures.

It will not, I am confident, revive an inflationary spiral or adversely affect our balance of payments. If the economy today were operating close to capacity levels with little unemployment, then we would oppose tax reductions as irresponsible and inflationary — and we would not hesitate to recommend a tax increase, if that were necessary. But our resources and manpower are not being fully utilized, the general level of prices has been remarkably stable, and increased competition — both at home and abroad — along with increased productivity, will help keep both prices and wages within appropriate limits. The same is true of our balance of payments.

While rising demand will expand imports, new investment in more efficient productive facilities will aid exports, and a new economic climate could both draw capital from abroad and keep capital here at home. It will also put us in a better position, if necessary, to use monetary tools to help our international accounts. But most importantly, confidence in the dollar in the long run rests on confidence in America, in our ability to meet our economic commitments and reach our economic goals.

But what concerns most Americans about a tax cut is not the deficit in our balance of payments, but the deficit in our federal budget. Therefore, the Government should neither postpone our tax cut plans nor cut into essential national security programs. Our true choice is not between tax reduction, on the one hand, and the avoidance of large federal deficits on the other. It is increasingly clear that no matter what party is in power, so long as our national security needs keep rising, an economy hampered by restrictive tax rates will never produce enough revenues to balance our budget — just as it will never produce enough jobs or enough profits. Surely the lesson of the last decade is that budget deficits are not caused by just wild-eyed spenders, but also by slow economic growth and periodic recessions, and any new recession would break all deficit records.

In short, it is a paradoxical truth that tax rates are too high today and tax revenues are too low and the soundest way to raise the revenues in the long run is to cut the rates now. The experiences of a number of European countries and Japan have borne this out. This country's own experience with tax reduction in the past has borne this out. And the reason is that only full employment can balance the budget, and tax reduction can pave the way to full employment. The purpose of cutting taxes now is not to incur a larger budget deficit, but to achieve the more prosperous, expanding economy which can bring about a balanced budget, and even a budget surplus. I repeat: our practical choice is not between a tax-cut deficit and a budgetary surplus. It is between two kinds of deficits: a chronic deficit of inertia, as the unwanted result of inadequate revenues and a restricted economy, or a temporary deficit of transition, resulting from a tax cut designed to boost the economy, increase tax revenues, and achieve, we believe — and we believe this can be done — a budget surplus. The first type of deficit is a sign of waste and weakness; the second reflects an investment in the future.

Nevertheless, as the Chairman of the House Ways and Means Committee pointed out, the size of the deficit is to be regarded with concern, and tax reduction must be accompanied, in his words, by "increased control of the rises in expenditures." This is precisely the course we intend to follow. This is not an easy task. During the past nine years, domestic civilian expenditures in the national government have risen at an average rate of more than seven-and-one-half percent. State and local government expenditures have risen at an annual rate of nine percent. Expenditures by the New York State government alone, for example, have risen in recent years at the rate of roughly ten percent per year. This budget will reflect, among other economies, a billion-dollar reduction in the postal deficit — and a saving[s] of billions of dollars from the cancellation of obsolete or unworkable weapons systems. The Secretary of Defense is undertaking a cost reduction program expected to save billions of dollars a year in the Department of Defense, cutting down on duplication and closing down nonessential installations. Other agencies must do the same.

In addition, as President, I would direct all heads of government departments and agencies to hold federal employment under the levels authorized by Congressional appropriations, to absorb through greater efficiency a substantial part of this year's federal pay increase, to achieve an increase in productivity which will enable the same amount of work to be done by less people, and to refrain from spending any unnecessary funds that were appropriated by the Congress.

It is this setting which makes federal tax reduction both possible and necessary next year. I do not underestimate the obstacles which the Congress will face in enacting such legislation. No one will be satisfied. Everyone will have his own approach, his own bill and his own reductions. A high order of restraint and determination will be required if the "possible" is not to wait on the "perfect." But a nation capable of marshaling these qualities in any dramatic threat to our security is surely capable, as a great free society, of meeting a slower and more complex threat to our economic vitality. This nation can afford to reduce taxes, and perhaps even afford a temporary increase in the deficit — but we cannot afford to do nothing. For on the strength of our free economy rests the hope of all free nations. I shall not fail that hope — for free men and free nations must prosper and they must prevail. *

*   John F. Kennedy–Economic Club of New York Speech delivered Dec. 14, 1962 in New York, New York

Chapter Fourteen
2025 VIRTUAL INAUGURAL SPEECH: THE NEW ECONOMIC NATIONALISM

"The true friend of property, the true conservative, is he who insists that property shall be the servant and not the master of the Country. The citizens of the United States must effectively control the mighty commercial forces which they have called into being."

- Theodore Roosevelt

Our country - this great Republic - means nothing unless it means the triumph of a real democracy, the triumph of popular government, and, in the long run, of an economic system under which each man shall be guaranteed the opportunity to show the best that there is in him. That is why the history of America is now the central feature of the history of the world; for the world has set its face hopefully toward our democracy. Therefore, my fellow citizens, each one of you carries on your shoulders not only the burden of doing well for the sake of your country, but the burden of doing well and of seeing that this nation does well for the sake of mankind and free people everywhere.

There have been two great crises in our country's history: first, when it was formed, and then, again, when it was perpetuated; and, in the second of these great crises-in the time of stress and strain which culminated in the Civil War. If this Republic had been founded only to be split asunder into fragments when the strain came, then the judgment of the world would have been that the work of our Founding Fathers was not worth doing. In name we had the Declaration of Independence in 1776; but we gave the lie by our acts to the words of the Declaration of Independence; and words count for nothing except insofar as they represent acts. This is true everywhere; but it should be truest of all in political life.

> *"A broken promise is bad enough in private life. It is worse in the field of politics. No man is worth his salt in public life who makes on the stump a pledge which he does not keep after election; and, if he makes such a pledge and does not keep it, hunt him out of public life." –*
> *Theodore Roosevelt*

I care for the great deeds of the past chiefly as spurs to drive us onward in the present. I speak of the men of the past partly that they may be honored by our praise of them, but more that they may serve as examples for the future. Even in ordinary times there are very few of us who do not see the problems of life as through a glass, darkly; and when the glass is clouded by the murk of furious popular passion, the vision of the best and the bravest is dimmed.

It is of little use for us to pay lip-service to the mighty men of the past unless we sincerely endeavor to apply to the problems of the present precisely the qualities which in other crises enabled the men of that day to meet those crises. Under the lead of

Abraham Lincoln, faced and solved the great problems of the nineteenth century, while, at the same time, these same good people nervously shrink from, or frantically denounce, those who are trying to meet the problems of today in the spirit which was accountable for the successful solution of the problems of Lincoln's time. Of that generation of men to whom we owe so much, the man to whom we owe most is, of course, Lincoln. Part of our debt to him is because he forecast our present struggle and saw the way out. He said:

> *"I hold that while man exists it is his duty to improve not only his own condition, but to assist in ameliorating mankind."*

And again:

> *"Labor is prior to, and independent of, capital. Capital is only the fruit of labor, and could never have existed if labor had not first existed. Labor is the superior of capital, and deserves much the higher consideration."*

If that remark was original with me, I should be even more strongly denounced as a Communist agitator than I shall be anyhow. It is Lincoln's. I am only quoting it; and that is one side; that is the side the capitalist should hear. Now, let the working man hear his side.

> *"Capital has its rights, which are as worthy of protection as any other rights. Nor should this lead to a war upon the owners of property. Property is the fruit of labor; . . . property is desirable; is a positive good in the world."*

And then comes a thoroughly Lincoln-like sentence:

> *"Let not him who is houseless pull down the house of another, but let him work diligently and build one for himself, thus by example assuring that his own shall be safe from violence when built."*

It seems to me that, in these words, Lincoln took substantially the attitude that we ought to take; he showed the proper sense of proportion in his relative estimates of capital and labor, of human rights and property rights. Above all, in this speech, as in many others, he taught a lesson in wise kindliness and charity; an indispensable lesson to us of today. But this wise kindliness and charity never weakened his arm or numbed his heart. We cannot afford weakly to blind ourselves to the actual conflict which faces us today. The issue is joined, and we must fight or fail.

In every wise struggle for human betterment one of the main objects, and often the only object, has been to achieve in large measure equality of opportunity. In the struggle for this great end, nations rise from barbarism to civilization, and through it people press forward from one stage of enlightenment to the next. One of the chief factors in progress is the destruction of special privilege. The essence of any struggle for healthy liberty has always been, and must always be, to take from some one man or class of men the right to enjoy power, wealth, or position, or immunity, which has not been earned by service to his or their fellows. That is what we strive for now.

At many stages in the advance of humanity, this conflict between the men who possess more than they have earned and the men who have earned more than they possess is the central condition of progress. In our day it appears as the struggle of freemen to gain and hold the right of self-government as against the special interests, who twist the methods of free government into machinery for defeating the popular will. At every stage, and under all circumstances, the essence of the struggle is to equalize opportunity, destroy privilege, and give to the life and citizenship of every individual the highest possible value both to himself and to the commonwealth. Practical equality of opportunity for all citizens, when we achieve it, will have two great results. First, every man will have a fair chance to make of himself all that in him lies; to reach the highest point to which his capacities, unassisted by special privilege of his own and unhampered by the special privilege of others, can carry him, and to get for himself and his family substantially what he has earned. Second, equality of opportunity means that the commonwealth will get from every citizen the highest service of which he is capable. No man who carries the burden of the special privileges of another can give to the Country that service to which it is fairly entitled.

I stand for the square deal. But when I say that I am for the square deal, I mean not merely that I stand for fair play under the present rules of the game, but that I stand for having those rules changed so as to work for a more substantial equality of opportunity and of reward for equally good service. When I say I want a square deal for the poor man, I do not mean that I want a square deal for the man who remains poor because he has not got the energy to work for himself.

This means that our government, National and State, must be freed from the sinister influence or control of special interests. The great special business interests too often control and corrupt the men and methods of government for their own profit. We must drive the special interests out of politics. That is one of our tasks today. Every special interest is entitled to justice - full, fair, and complete - and, now, mind you, if there were any attempt by mob-violence to plunder and work harm to the special interest, whatever it may be, that I most dislike, and the wealthy man, whomsoever he may be, for whom I have the greatest contempt, I would fight for him. And you would too, if you were worth your salt. He should have justice. For every special interest is entitled to justice, but not one is entitled to a vote in Congress, to a voice on the bench, or to representation in any public office. The Constitution guarantees protection to property, and we must make that promise good. But it does not give the right of suffrage to any corporation.

The true friend of property, the true conservative, is he who insists that property shall be the servant and not the master of the Country; who insists that the creature of man's making shall be the servant and not the master of the man who made it. The citizens of the United States must effectively control the mighty commercial forces which they have called into being. There can be no effective control of corporations while their political activity remains. To put an end to it will be neither a short nor an easy task, but it can be done.

We must have complete and effective publicity of corporate affairs, so that the people may know beyond peradventure whether the corporations obey the law and whether their management entitles them to the confidence of the public. It is necessary that laws should be passed to prohibit the use of corporate funds directly or indirectly for political purposes; it is still more necessary that such laws should be thoroughly enforced. Corporate expenditures for political purposes, and especially such expenditures by public-service corporations, have supplied one of the principal sources of corruption in our political affairs.

I believe that the officers, and, especially, the directors, of corporations should be held personally responsible when any corporation breaks the law. There is a wide-spread belief among our people that the special interests are too influential. Probably this is true of both the big special interests and the little special interests. These methods have put a premium on selfishness, and, naturally, the selfish big interests have gotten more than their smaller, though equally selfish, brothers. The duty of Congress is to provide a method by which the interest of the whole people shall be all that receives consideration.

The absence of effective State, and, especially, national,

restraint upon unfair money-getting has tended to create a small class of enormously wealthy and economically powerful men, whose chief object is to hold and increase their power. The prime need to is to change the conditions which enable these men to accumulate power which it is not for the general welfare that they should hold or exercise. We grudge no man a fortune which represents his own power and sagacity, when exercised with entire regard to the welfare of his fellows. Again, comrades over there, take the lesson from your own experience. Not only did you not grudge, but you gloried in the promotion of the great generals who gained their promotion by leading their army to victory.

So it is with us. We grudge no man a fortune in civil life if it is honorably obtained and well used. It is not even enough that it should have been gained without doing damage to the community. We should permit it to be gained only so long as the gaining represents benefit to the community. This, I know, implies a policy of a far more active governmental interference with social and economic conditions in this country than we have yet had, but I think we have got to face the fact that such an increase in governmental control is now necessary.

No man should receive a dollar unless that dollar has been fairly earned. Every dollar received should represent a dollar's worth of service rendered - not gambling in stocks, but service rendered. The really big fortune, the swollen fortune, by the mere fact of its size, acquires qualities which differentiate it in kind as well as in degree from what is possessed by men of relatively small means. Therefore, I believe in a graduated income tax on big fortunes, and in another tax which is far more easily collected and far more effective - a graduated inheritance tax on big fortunes, properly safeguarded against evasion, and increasing rapidly in amount with the size of the estate.

The people of the United States suffer from periodical financial panics to a degree substantially unknown to the other nations, which approach us in financial strength. There is no reason why we should suffer what they escape. It is of profound importance that our financial system should be promptly investigated, and so thoroughly and effectively revised as to make it certain that hereafter our currency will no longer fail at critical times to meet our needs.

It is hardly necessary for me to repeat that I believe in an efficient army and a navy large enough to secure for us abroad that respect which is the surest guaranty of peace. A word of special warning to my fellow citizens who are as progressive as I hope I am. I want them to keep up their interest in our international affairs; and I want them also continually to remember Uncle Sam's interests abroad. Justice and fair dealings among nations rest upon principles identical with those which control justice and fair dealing among the individuals of which nations are composed, with the vital exception that each nation must do its own part in international police work. If you get into trouble here, you can call for the police; but if Uncle Sam gets into trouble, he has got to be his own policeman, and I want to see him strong enough to encourage the peaceful aspirations of other people in connection with us.

I believe in national friendships and heartiest goodwill to all nations; but national friendships, like those between men, must be founded on respect as well as on liking, on forbearance as well as upon trust. I should be heartily ashamed of any American who did not try to make the American government act as justly toward the other nations in international relations as he himself would act toward any individual in private relations. I should be heartily ashamed to see us wrong a weaker power, and I should hang my head forever if we tamely suffered wrong from a stronger power.

Of conservation, I shall speak more at length elsewhere. Conservation means development as much as it does protection. I recognize the right and duty of this generation to develop and use the natural resources of our land; but I do not recognize the right to waste them, or to rob, by wasteful use, the generations that come after us. I ask nothing of the nation except that it so behave as each farmer here behaves with reference to his own children. That farmer is a poor creature who skins the land and leaves it worthless to his children. The farmer is a good farmer who, having enabled the land to support himself and to provide for the education of his children, leaves it to them a little better than he found it himself. I believe the same thing of a nation.

Moreover, I believe that the natural resources must be used for the benefit of all our people, and not monopolized for the benefit of the few, and here again is another case in which I am accused of taking a revolutionary attitude. People forget now that one hundred years ago there were public men of good character who advocated the nation selling its public lands in great quantities, so that the nation could get the most money out of it, and giving it to the men who could cultivate it for their own uses. We took the proper democratic ground that the land should be granted in small sections to the men who were actually to till it and live on it. Now, with the water-power, with the forests, with the mines, we are brought face to face with the fact that there are many people who will go with us in conserving the resources only if they are to be allowed to exploit them for their benefit.

That is one of the fundamental reasons why the special interests should be driven out of politics. Of all the questions which can come before this nation, short of the actual preservation of its existence in a great war, there is none which compares in importance with the great central task of leaving this land even a better land for our descendants than it is for us, and training them into a better race to inhabit the land and pass it on. Conservation is a great moral issue, for it involves the patriotic duty of ensuring the safety and continuance of the nation. Let me add that the health and vitality of our people are at least as well worth conserving as their forests, waters, lands, and minerals, and in this great work the national government must bear a most important part.

Nothing is truer than that excess of every kind is followed by reaction; a fact which should be pondered by reformer and reactionary alike. We are face to face with new conceptions of the relations of property to human welfare, chiefly because certain advocates of the rights of property as against the rights of men have been pushing their claims too far. The man who wrongly holds that every human right is secondary to his profit must now give way to the advocate of human welfare, who rightly maintains that every man holds his property subject to the general right of the community to regulate its use to whatever degree the public welfare may require it. But I think we may go still further.

The right to regulate the use of wealth in the public interest is universally admitted. Let us admit also the right to regulate the terms and conditions of labor, which is the chief element of wealth, directly in the interest of the common good. The fundamental thing to do for every man is to give him a chance to reach a place in which he will make the greatest possible contribution to the public welfare. Understand what I say there. Give him a chance, not push him up if he will not be pushed. Help any man who stumbles; if he lies down, it is a poor job to try to carry him; but if he is a worthy man, try your best to see that he gets a chance to show the worth that is in him. No man can be a good citizen unless he has a wage more than sufficient to cover the bare cost of living, and hours of labor short enough so after his day's work is done, he will have time and energy to bear his share in the management of the community, to help in carrying the general load. We keep countless men from being good citizens by the conditions of life which we surround them. If I could ask but one thing of my fellow countrymen, my request would be that, whenever they go in for reform, they remember the two sides, and that they always exact justice from one side as much as from the other. I have small use for the public servant who can always see and denounce the corruption of the capitalist, but who cannot persuade himself, especially before election, to say a word about lawless mob-violence. And I have equally small use for the man, be he a judge on the bench or editor of a great paper, or wealthy and influential private citizen, who can see clearly enough and denounce the lawlessness of mob-violence, but whose eyes are closed so that he is blind when the question is one of corruption of business on a gigantic scale. Also, remember what I said about excess in reformer and reactionary alike. If the reactionary man, who thinks of nothing but the rights of property, could have his way, he would bring about a revolution; and one of my chief fears in connection with progress comes because I do not want to see our people, for lack of proper leadership, compelled to follow men whose intentions are excellent, but whose eyes are a little too wild to make it really safe to trust them.

National efficiency has many factors. It is a necessary result of the principle of conservation widely applied. In the end, it will determine our failure or success as a nation. National efficiency has to do, not only with natural resources and with men, but it is equally concerned with institutions. The State must be made efficient for the work which concerns only the people of the State; and the nation for that which concerns all the people. I do not ask for the over centralization; but I do ask that we work in a spirit of broad and far-reaching nationalism where we work for what concerns our people as a whole. We are all Americans. Our common interests are as broad as the continent. The National Government belongs to the whole American people, and where the whole American people are interested, that interest can be guarded effectively only by the National Government. The betterment which we seek must be accomplished, I believe, mainly through the National Government.

The American people are right in demanding that New Economic Nationalism, without which we cannot hope to deal with new problems. The New Economic Nationalism puts the national need before sectional or personal advantage. It is impatient of the utter confusion that results from local legislatures attempting to treat national issues as local issues. It is still more impatient of the impotence which springs from over division of governmental powers, the impotence which makes it possible for local selfishness or for legal cunning, hired by wealthy special interests, to bring national activities to a deadlock. This New Economic Nationalism regards the executive power as the steward of the public welfare. It demands of the judiciary that it shall be interested primarily in human welfare rather than in property, just as it demands that the representative body shall represent all the people rather than any one class or section of the people.

I believe in shaping the ends of government to protect property as well as human welfare. Normally, and in the long run, the ends are the same; but whenever the alternative must be faced, I am for men and not for property. I am far from underestimating the importance of corporate profits; but I rank dividends below human character. Again, I do not have any sympathy with the reformer who says he does not care for corporate profits. Of course, economic welfare is necessary, for a man must pull his own weight and be able to support his family.

I know well that the reformers must not bring upon the people economic ruin, or the reforms themselves will go down in the ruin. But we must be ready to face temporary disaster, whether or not brought on by those who will war against us to the knife. Those who oppose reform will do well to remember that ruin in its worst form is inevitable if our national life brings us nothing better than swollen fortunes for the few and the triumph in both politics and business of a sordid and selfish materialism.

If our political institutions were perfect, they would absolutely prevent the political domination of money in any part of our affairs. We need to make our political representatives more quickly and sensitively responsive to the people whose servants they are. More direct action by the people in their own affairs under proper safeguards is vitally necessary. The direct primary is a step in this direction, if it is associated with a corrupt- services act effective to prevent the advantage of the man willing recklessly and unscrupulously to spend money over his more honest competitor. It is particularly important that all moneys received or expended for campaign purposes should be publicly accounted for, not only after election, but before election as well. Political action must be made simpler, easier, and freer from confusion for every citizen. I believe that the prompt removal of unfaithful or incompetent public servants should be made easy and sure in whatever way experience shall show to be most expedient in any given class of cases.

One of the fundamental necessities in a representative government such as ours is to make certain that the men to whom the people delegate their power shall serve the people by whom they are elected, and not the special interests. I believe that every national officer, elected or appointed, should be forbidden to perform any service or receive any compensation, directly or indirectly, from interstate corporations; and a similar provision could not fail to be useful within the States.

The object of government is the welfare of the people. The material progress and prosperity of a nation are desirable chiefly so long as they lead to the moral and material welfare of all good citizens. Just in proportion as the average man and woman are honest, capable of sound judgment and high ideals, active in public affairs, but first of all, sound in their home, and the father and mother of healthy children whom they bring up well, just so far, and no farther, we may count our civilization a success. We must have - I believe we have already - a genuine and permanent moral awakening, without which no wisdom of legislation or administration really means anything; and, on the other hand, we must try to secure the social and economic legislation without which any improvement due to purely moral agitation is necessarily evanescent. In the last analysis, therefore, vitally necessary though it was to have the right kind of organization and the right kind of leadership, it was even more vitally necessary that the average soldier should have the fighting edge, the right character.

So it is in our civil life. No matter how honest and decent we are in our private lives, if we do not have the right kind of law and the right kind of administration of the law, we cannot go forward as a nation. That is imperative; but it must be an addition to, and not a substitute for, the qualities that make us good citizens. In the last analysis, the most important elements in any man's career must be the sum of those qualities which, in the aggregate, we speak of as character. If he has not got it, then no law that the wit of man can devise, no administration of the law by the boldest and strongest executive, will avail to help him. We must have the right kind of character - character that makes a man, first of all, a good man in the home, a good father, and a good husband - that makes a man a good neighbor. You must have that, and, then, in addition, you must have the kind of law and the kind of administration of the law which will give to those qualities in the private citizen the best possible chance for development. The prime problem of our nation is to get the right type of good citizenship, and, to get it, we must have progress, and our public servants must be genuinely progressive. *

---

*   Theodore Roosevelt – The New Nationalism Speech delivered August 31, 1910 Osawatomie, Kansas

Chapter Fifteen
ECONOMIC STRATEGY FOR THE FUTURE

*"I predict future happiness for Americans, if
they can prevent the government from wasting
the labors of the people under the pretense of
taking care of them."*

- Thomas Jefferson

Sharp change in present economic policy is an absolute necessity. The problems of inflation, deflation and slow growth, of falling standards of living and declining productivity, of high government spending but an inadequate flow of funds for an almost endless litany of economic ills, large and small, are severe, they are not intractable. Having been produced by government policy, they can be redressed by a change in policy.

The new reports that you commissioned during the campaign are now available. They contain an impressive array of concrete recommendations for action. More than that, the able people who served on the Task Forces are available to provide further detail and backup information to you or your designees. We all want to help and you can count on enthusiastic and conscientious effort from all of us in the movement. Your Coordinating Committee has reviewed the Task Force reports. With due allowance for some differences in view about particulars and relative importance, we have found that they offer a substantial base for action by you and the team you assemble. We focus here on guiding principles, on priorities and linkages among policy areas, and on the problem of getting action. You have identified in the campaign the key issues and lines of policy necessary to restore hope and confidence in a better economic future:

- *Reestablish stability in the purchasing power of the dollar.*

- *Achieve a widely-shared prosperity through real growth in jobs, investment, and productivity.*

- *Devote the resources needed for a strong defense, and accomplish the goal of releasing the creative forces of entrepreneurship, management, and labor by:*

- *Restraining government spending.*

- *Reducing the burden of taxation and regulation.*

- *Conducting monetary policy in a steady manner, directed toward eliminating inflation while avoiding deflation and recession.*

This amounts to emphasis on fundamentals for the full four years, as the key to a flourishing economy.

Guiding Principles

The essence of good policy is good strategy. Some strategic principles can guide your new administration as it charts its course.

- ***Timing and preparation are critical aspects of strategy.***

The fertile moment may come suddenly and evaporate as quickly. The administration that is well prepared is ready to act when the time is ripe. The transition period and the early months of the new administration are a particularly fertile period. The opportunity to set the tone for your Administration must be seized by putting the fundamental policies into place immediately and decisively.

- ***The need for a long-term point of view is essential to allow for the time, the coherence, and the predictability so necessary for success.***

This long-term view is as important for day-to-day problem solving as for the making of large policy decisions. Most decisions in government are made in the process of responding to problems of the moment. The danger is that this daily firefighting can lead the policy- maker farther and farther from his goals. A clear sense of guiding strategy makes it possible to move in the desired direction in the unending process of contending with issues of the day. Many failures of government can be traced to an attempt to solve problems piecemeal. The resulting patchwork of *ad hoc* solutions often makes such fundamental goals as military strength, price stability, and economic growth more difficult to achieve.

- ***Central problems that your Administration must face are linked by their substance and their root causes.***

Measures adopted to deal with one problem will inevitably have effects on others. It is as important to recognize these interrelationships as it is to recognize the individual problems themselves.

- ***Consistency in policy is critical to effectiveness. Individuals and business enterprises plan on a long-range basis.***

They need to have an environment in which they can conduct their affairs with confidence.

- ***Specific policies as well as long-term strategy should be announced publicly.***

The Administration should commit itself to their achievement, and should seek Congressional commitment to them as well. Then the public, as well as the government, knows what to expect.

- ***The administration should be candid with the public.***

It should not over-promise, especially with respect to the speed with which the policies adopted can achieve the desired results.

Seizing the Initiative

The fundamental areas of economic strategy concern the budget, taxation, regulation, and monetary policy. Prompt action in each of these areas is essential to establish both your resolve and your capacity to achieve your goals.

Budget

Your most immediate concern upon assuming the duties of the President will be to convince the financial markets and the public at large that your cut-spending, lower tax, strong dollar, anti-inflation policy is more than just rhetoric. The public, especially the financial community, are skeptical and need a startling demonstration of resolve. Many question the seriousness of a sizeable cut in budget outlays. Credible FY 2025 and 2026 budgets which do that without ambiguity would evoke an extraordinary response in the financial markets, and set the stage for a successful assault on inflation and a decline in mortgage and other interest rates.

The FY 2025 Budget will be almost four months along by the time you take office and a FY 2026 Budget will have been submitted for consideration by the Congress. There are now estimates of alarming increases in these swollen budgets. Prompt and strong action is necessary if these budgets are to be brought under control, as they must be. The nation can no longer afford governmental business as usual. It has been over four years since the Senate has passed a budget; and the CBO says the Country is headed over a fiscal cliff.

The formal budget alone is far from the whole story, though it is visible and important. Off-budget financing and government guarantees mount and expand programs through the use of the government's borrowing capacity, draining the nation's resources without being adequately recorded in the formal spending totals. In addition, the mandating of private expenditures for government purposes has gained momentum as the spotlight has illuminated direct spending. These mandates are also a clear call by government on the nation's resources. Efforts to control spending should be comprehensive; otherwise, good work in one area will be negated in another. And these efforts should be part of the Administration's development of a long-term strategy for the detailed shape of the budget, four or more years into the future.

The Task Force has identified an extensive and promising array of areas for potential savings, but it will be up to your Administration and the Congress to do the job. It takes top-notch people to do it. We recommend that:

- *A Budget Director, permanent or pro tem, be chosen and set to work now.*

- *A small team from OMB be assembled explicitly to work with the newly designated Director.*

- *The Director's recommendations be a part of your discussion with Cabinet appointees as these appointments are made.*

Amendments calling for dramatic reductions in the FY 2025 Budget should be submitted to the Congress within the first week of your Administration. A thoroughly revised FY 2026 Budget provides even greater opportunities for large further reductions, and this budget should be submitted as soon as possible. You should call for immediate cuts in government agency payrolls as much as 80% of each agency should be cut.

Finally, it has become all too evident in recent years that current budget procedures are biased in an expansionary direction. The Congressional budget process defined by the Budget Act of 1974 and its subsequent amendments have failed to achieve their purpose of removing the "runaway" bias. We therefore recommend a presidential task force to develop new techniques which can help to rein in the growth of federal outlays and federal spending. It should re-examine the presidential line-item veto, renewed presidential power to refrain from spending appropriated funds, and other initiatives to hold down spending. This task force should report to you within two months.

Tax Policy

Tax policy is properly the province of your Secretary of the Treasury. The making of that appointment should have a high priority so that important work can go forward. The Task Force provides the materials needed to pose the issues to you in concrete form and to translate your decisions into a proposal to the Congress. This proposal should be presented early in the new administration in tandem with other key elements of your economic program. It should embody the main thrust of tax policy for the whole of your first term, not simply for the year 2025. The key ingredients should be your proposed cut in personal income tax rates, simplification and liberalization of business depreciation and a cut in effective taxes on capital gains by keeping the Bush tax cuts in place. Consistent with your proposals earlier this year, the effective date for these reductions should be January 1, 2025.

Other key proposals are tax incentives for the establishment of enterprise zones in the inner cities and such other items as tuition tax credits so people can tax deduct college tuition, and the elimination of all of the anti-growth tax penalties and regulations put in by the last administration. Once again, the biggest step is making a new Commissioner of the IRS. Currently the Tax Code is one volume of Code and five volumes of Regulations. Each volume is larger than the King James Bible. The Code is Congress' fault. The five volumes of Regulations are the IRS's fault. Make a new Commissioner and let him cut the Regulations to one volume.

Regulation

The current regulatory overburden must be removed from the economy. Equally important, the flood of new and extremely burdensome regulations that the agencies are now issuing or planning to issue must be drastically curtailed. The Task Force sets out the needed blueprint for personnel selection, immediate administrative action, and legislation. Again, the key to action is a knowledgeable and forceful individual to develop and coordinate strategy and to form a team to carry it out. Such an appointment should be made promptly, with the expectation that the effort would carry forward through the transition for at least a year into your Administration. Your appointee and his team should be located within the Executive Office of the President. Achieving regulatory reform will take informed, strong, and skillful work with the Congress, as well as with those in charge of departmental and agency regulatory efforts. The person heading up this effort will require your continued, wholehearted support.

Many of our economic problems today stem from the large and increasing proportion of economic decisions being made through the political process rather than the market process. An important step to demonstrate your determination to rely on markets would be the prompt end of wage and price guidelines and elimination of the Council on Wage and Price Stability, along with other federal agencies such as the Departments of Education, Energy, Labor and Commerce, along with terribly ineffective agencies like the Environmental Protection Agency. If not entirely eliminated, their budgets and payrolls should be immediately cut by 80%. To advance the entire regulatory effort—both to galvanize public support and to strengthen the positions of Administration appointees— we urge you to issue a message on regulatory reform in tandem with the budget and tax messages. The message should call upon state and local governments to launch similar regulatory reform efforts—as a few have already done. The states and cities are necessarily cutting their budgets or facing bankruptcy. We cannot allow America to go over a fiscal cliff.

Energy

The battle between government regulation and the private market is nowhere more apparent than in energy, where the market has a decisive comparative advantage. Governmental intrusion into energy production and use provides a glaring example of how regulation costs us all dearly. Alternatives to imported oil exist here in the United States. As the Task Force emphasizes, market pricing and market incentives will accelerate the development of these alternatives, just as surely as present regulations and the politicization of this field inhibit them. Its recommendations and the issues it poses for careful review cover the energy field in a comprehensive manner and deserve immediate attention. Look at North Dakota and Alaska. Look at the new uses of sugar-based, not corn-based, fuels.

We recommend, also, that you promptly exercise the discretion granted to the President to remove the price controls on crude oil and petroleum products and increase margin requirements to stop the speculators. This decisive action will eliminate at once the regulatory apparatus administering the entitlements program, and discourage continued efforts by special interests, to prevent or slow down decontrol and deregulation. Also, the Natural Gas Act should be repealed so that all natural gas prices are decontrolled. These measures are particularly urgent because the uncertainty of our Middle East oil supplies, dramatized by the potential wars in the Middle East, makes it all the more necessary to get the earliest possible incentive effect of free market pricing.

The Department of Energy has become a large and unmanageable institution with a variety of programs ranging from essential to useless. The essential functions should be transferred and the Department eliminated. This should be the main task of your Secretary of Energy. The first year the payroll and budget should be cut by 80%, and the entire department eliminated by the second year of your first term.

Monetary Policy

A steady and moderate rate of monetary growth is an essential requirement both to control inflation and to provide a healthy environment for economic growth. We have not had such a policy. The rate of monetary growth declined sharply in the early months of 2020, and rose rapidly in recent months. These wide fluctuations are adversely affecting economic conditions and may continue to do so for some time.

The Task Force emphasizes that the attainment of a proper monetary policy deserves the very highest priority and that such a monetary policy can be achieved through effective use by the Fed of its existing powers. The Task Force also brings out the relationship of monetary policy to budgetary and other economic policies. The Federal Reserve is an independent agency. However, independence should not mean lack of accountability for what it does. In practice, independence has not meant that the Federal Reserve is immune to Presidential and Congressional influence. The problem is how to assume accountability while preserving independence. We suggest that you:

- *Request the Fed to state targets for monetary growth year by year for the next five years that in its opinion will end inflation. Influential members of relevant committees of Congress have already urged the Fed to specify such long-term targets.*

- *Assure the Fed that you will propose and fight for fiscal and other policies compatible with the elimination of inflation.*

- *Improve the procedures for coordinating Federal Reserve monetary policy with the economic policies of the Administration and the Congress and support Congressional efforts to monitor the Fed's performance and to recommend changes in the procedures that could improve performance.*

With these fundamentals in place, the American people will respond. As the conviction grows that the policies will be sustained in a consistent manner over an extended period, the response will quicken. And a healthy U. S. economy, as the Task Force states, will restore the credibility of our dollar on world markets, contribute significantly to smoother operation of the international economy, and enhance America's strength in the world. America needs a strong dollar and so does the World. We need to restore fiscal integrity as well as monetary integrity.

Organizing for Action

The activities of a wide variety of departments, agencies, and other units of government within the Executive Branch impinge on economic policy. But, the flow of economic events does not recognize organizational lines. The economy itself operates as a system in which constituent parts are linked, sometimes tightly. The combination of interwoven problems and disparate organizations means that, in the process of policy formulation and implementation, some people high in your administration must identify the central ideas and problems and devise a strategy for dealing with them. Your leadership is essential to this effort.

One arrangement that has worked well in the past is for the Secretary of Treasury to be the chief coordinator and spokesman on economic policy, domestic and international. To carry out this mandate effectively, the Secretary should be one of your key staff members as well as a departmental head with a White House title and office. Since economic developments are often closely related to security, the Secretary should be a member of the National Security Council. For this coordinating role, an Economic Policy Board, with comprehensive membership, should be established; it should meet regularly and be the avenue through which economic issues come to your Executive of the Cabinet and to your desk. The Council of Economic Advisers might suitably provide the secretariat for this group. None of this matters, however, if you do not have strong leadership at the post of the Commissioner of the IRS. Without a strong leader at the helm, tax reform is impossible. With a strong Commissioner, he can reform the collection of taxes in such a way that the government gets more revenue with less taxpayer stress. The IRS can be kinder, gentler, and taxpayer friendly; a system that works.

Maintaining a Steady Course

Our final point is our most important one. The success of your economic policy will be a direct reflection of your ability to maintain a steady course over your full first term. Rough times will come and unexpected crises, some small, some of great moment, will arise. Sustained effort through these testing times means that public understanding and support are essential. Of equal and related importance is the understanding and support of the Congress. This last task—gaining understanding and support of Congress—is of crucial importance. As a result of the voting on November 3, the new Congress, we are convinced, will be more cooperative on economic and financial issues. That cooperation will be fostered if, during the transition, the Secretary of the Treasury (designate) consults intensively with key members of Congress on the design and implementation of your economic policies.

You have emphasized in your successful campaign precisely the strategy set forth in this document. In moving to implement it, you will be doing what the people voted for. Every effort must be made to maintain and broaden your base of support by improving public understanding and by close cooperation with the Congress. Cabinet officers and others in your administration can help in these tasks. Their ability to do so should be one important criterion in their selection. At the end of the day, however, the burden of leadership falls on you: leadership to chart the course ahead; leadership to persuade that your course is the one to take; leadership to stay on course, whatever way political winds may blow. Through effective advocacy of the sharp changes so sorely needed, your leadership has brought us to this long-hoped-for opportunity at a critical moment for the nation. Your leadership can maintain this advocacy in the convincing manner necessary for a successful outcome. *

---

* Excerpts taken from November 16, 1980 memo to President Elect Ronald Reagan entitled: "Economic Strategy for the Reagan Administration."

Appendix I

The Road to Serfdom (in Cartoons)

Originally published in *Look* magazine

Reproduced from a booklet published by
General Motors, Detroit, in the 'Thought Starter' series (no. 118)

❶

War forces "national planning"

To permit total mobilization of your country's economy, you gladly surrender many freedoms. You know regimentation was forced by your country's enemies.

❷

Many want "planning" to stay . . .
Arguments for a "peace production
board" are heard before the war
ends. Wartime "planners" who want
to stay in power, encourage the idea.

3

The "Planners" promise Utopias . . . .

A rosy plan for farmers goes well in rural areas, a plan for industrial workers is popular in cities—and so on. Many new "planners" are elected to office

❹

but they can't agree on ONE Utopia

With peace, a new legislature meets;
but "win the war" unity is gone. The
"planners" nearly come to blows. Each
has his own pet plan, won't budge.

And citizens can't agree either . . . .

When the "planners" finally patch up a temporary plan months later, citizens in turn disagree. What the farmer likes, the factory worker doesn't like.

6

"Planners" hate to force agreement . . .

Most "national planners" are well-meaning idealists, balk at any use of force. They hope for some miracle of public agreement as to their patchwork plan.

They try to "sell" the plan to all . . .

In an unsuccessful effort to educate people to uniform views, "planners" establish a giant propaganda machine —*which coming dictator will find handy.*

The gullible do find agreement . . . .

Meanwhile, growing national confusion leads to protest meetings. The least educated—thrilled and convinced by fiery oratory, form a party.

9

Confidence in "planners" fades . . . .

The more that the "planners" improvise,
the greater the disturbance to normal
business. Everybody suffers. People now
feel—rightly—that "planners" can't get
things done!

The "strong man" is given power . . .

In desperation, "planners" authorize the new party leader to hammer out a plan and force its obedience. Later, they'll dispense with him—or *so they think.*

The party takes over the country . . .

By now, confusion is so great that obedience to the new leader must be obtained at all costs. Maybe you join the party yourself to aid national unity.

A *negative* aim welds party unity . . .

Early step of all dictators is to inflame the majority in common cause against some scapegoat minority. In Germany, the negative aim was *Anti-Semitism*.

No one opposes the leader's plan . . .
It would be suicide; new secret police are
ruthless. Ability to force obedience always
becomes the No. 1 virtue in the "planned
state." Now *all* freedom is gone.

Your profession is "planned" . . . .

The wider job choice promised by now defunct "planners" turns out to be a tragic farce. "Planners" never have delivered, never will be able to.

Your wages are "planned" . . . .

Divisions of the wage scale must be arbitrary and rigid. Running a "planned state" from central headquarters is *clumsy, unfair, inefficient.*

Your thinking is "planned" . . . .

In the dictatorship, unintentionally
created by the planners, there is no room
for difference of opinion. Posters,
radio, press—*all tell you the same lies!*

17

Your recreation is "planned" . . . .
It is no coincidence that sports and
amusements have been carefully
"planned" in all regimented nations.
Once started, "planners" can't stop.

Your disciplining is "planned" . . . .

If you're fired from your job, it's apt to
be by a firing squad. What used to be an
error has now become a *crime* against
the state. ***Thus ends the road to serfdom!***